FLORIDA
Cook Book

GOLDENWEST
PUBLISHERS

Acknowledgments
Special thanks to the Gulf Coast Heritage Association, Inc. for allowing us to include recipes from their cookbook, *Historic Spanish Point: Cooking Then and Now*. For further information, call 1-941-966-5214 or mail: Gulf Coast Heritage Association, Inc., P.O. Box 846m Osprey, Florida 34229.

Printed in the United States of America
5th Printing © 2007
ISBN13: 978-1-885590-55-8
ISBN10: 1-885590-55-5

Golden West Publishers
4113 N. Longview Ave.
Phoenix, AZ 85014, USA

(602) 265-4392
(800) 658-5830

For sample recipes for every Golden West cookbook, visit:
www.goldenwestpublishers.com

Introduction

Spanish explorers named this land La Florida, meaning Land of Flowers. Today Florida's natural beauty still attracts millions of visitors. Through the years Florida has developed into an inspiring blend of natural resources and commercial successes. Originally inhabited by Native Americans, explored by the Spaniards, and in more recent times developed by North Americans, Florida boasts a diverse cultural heritage, which includes European, African, Caribbean and Latin American influences.

You can't mention Florida without thinking of citrus—oranges, grapefruit, and tangerines, as well as many more exotic types, such kumquats. Florida is much more than citrus, offering seafood from two coasts—the Atlantic Ocean and the Gulf of Mexico—featuring delicacies such as shrimp, crab, clams, sea bass and swordfish. Florida is also one of the leading producers of beef in the United States, as well as strawberries, tomatoes and other agricultural products.

We invite you to savor the flavors of Florida!

Florida Facts

Size—22nd largest state with a area of 58,560 square miles
Population—14,916,000 (1998)
State Animal—Florida Panther
State Beverage—Orange Juice
State Bird—Mockingbird
State Capital—Tallahassee, capital since 1845
State Flower—Orange Blossom
Statehood—March 3,1845, the 27th state admitted to the Union
State Motto—In God We Trust
State Nickname—The Sunshine State
State Song—"Old Folks at Home" ("Suwannee River") by
Stephen Foster
State Freshwater Fish—Largemouth Bass
State Reptile—Alligator
State Saltwater Fish—Sailfish
State Shell—The Horse Conch
State Stone—Agatized Coral & Moonstone
State Saltwater Mammal—Manatee
State Tree—Sabal Palm

Some Famous Floridians

John James Audubon, ornithologist, artist; **Julian "Cannonball" Adderley**, jazz saxophonist; **Pat Boone**, singer; **Steve Carlton**, baseball player; **Bo Diddley**, singer; **Faye Dunaway**, actress; **Stepin Fetchit**, comedian/actor; **Robert Hemingway**, author: **Frances Langford**, singer; **Jim Morrison**, singer; **Osceola**, Seminole Indian leader; **Tom Petty**, singer; **Sidney Poitier**, actor; **Janet Reno**, U.S. Attorney General; **David Robinson**, basketball; **Don Sutton**, baseball player, **Norman E. Thargard**, astronaut; **Tennessee Williams**, playwright; **Ben Vereen**, actor

Useful Information

Tourist Information: 1-850-488-5607 or 1-888-735-2872
National Forest Information: Reservations 1-800-280-2267
Fishing Regulations: Freshwater 1-850-488-4676
                    Saltwater 1-850-488-7910

Table of Contents

Appetizers & Beverages

Crabmeat Delights

"We have so much seafood available in Florida, I thought this would be a great appetizer to appear in our state cookbook! I have made this recipe for thirty years."

Sylvia D. Owens—Williston

1/4 cup melted **Butter**
1 cup chopped **Green Onions**
1/4 cup chopped fresh **Parsley**
1 tbsp. minced **Garlic**
1/4 cup **Dry White Wine**

1lb. fresh **Lump Crabmeat,** drained
2 tbsp. **Mayonnaise**
1/8 tsp. **Paprika**
1/8 tsp. **Red Pepper**

In a large skillet, melt butter, add onion, parsley and garlic and sauté until onions are tender. Stir in wine and cook for 1 minute. Add crabmeat, stir, then remove mixture from heat. Stir in mayonnaise, paprika and red pepper and pour into a chafing dish. Serve with melba rounds or spoon mixture over fresh-baked biscuits. Yields 2-3 cups.

Gator Fritters

A tasty Florida recipe from Alligator Bob's Gourmet Alligator Cookbook

Robert N. Young—Alligator Bob's, Plant City

2 cups **Unbleached All-Purpose Flour**
1 cup chopped **Onion**
3 tbsp. chopped fresh **Parsley**
2 tbsp. chopped **Chives** or **Green Onions**
1 tbsp. chopped **Jalapeño Pepper**
3 cloves **Garlic**, chopped
2 tsp. chopped fresh **Thyme** or 1/2 tsp. dried **Thyme**

1 tsp. **Distilled White Vinegar**
1/2 tsp. **Baking Soda**
1 cup **Milk**
Alligator, any cut, chopped
Salt and **Pepper** to taste
8 oz. **Vegetable Oil**
2 **Limes,** cut into wedges

In a medium mixing bowl, combine the first 9 ingredients. Add milk and stir until mixture is smooth. Stir in alligator pieces and season generously with salt and pepper. Heat oil to 375 degrees in a deep iron skillet or heavy saucepan. Working in batches, scoop batter by heaping teaspoonfuls and carefully push off spoon into hot oil. Fry for 3 minutes or until golden brown. Drain on paper towels. Serve with lime wedges.

Did you Know?

About 10,000 Indians lived in Florida along the western coast when white men first reached its shores. They belonged to four main tribes. The Calusa and the Tequesta in the south were hunters and fishermen. The Timucua lived in the central and northeast region, and the Apalachee in the northwest were farmers and hunters.

Smoked Marlin Dip

"This recipe came from a Florida friend who now runs a Bed & Breakfast in Maine. It's a family favorite and perfect for parties."

Lea Ann Baker—Miami

1 smoked **Marlin Fillet**, or other smoked, meaty fish fillet
1 medium **Onion**, chopped
5 cloves **Garlic**, minced
1 package (8 oz.) **Cream Cheese**
10 dashes **Tabasco**® or more, to taste
White Pepper to taste
Milk
Mayonnaise

Cut fish fillet into small pieces, place in food processor or blender and chop. Mix in onion, garlic, cream cheese, Tabasco and pepper. Add milk and mayonnaise until mixture is spread-able but not too creamy. Serve with crackers.

Zesty Beef 'n' Bean Wedges

"This was a prize-winning recipe from the 1998 Florida Beef Cook-Off."

Polly Golden—Florida Beef Council, Kissimmee

1 lb. **Ground Round**
1 can (15 oz.) **Chili Hot Beans**, drained
1 cup **Cornbread Stuffing Mix** (Southwestern-Flavored)
1 tbsp. fresh **Lime Juice**
1/8 tsp. **Pepper**
1 cup shredded **Jalapeño Pepper Cheese**
1/4 cup sliced **Green Onions**
Lime Wedges, for garnish

Preheat oven to 375 degrees. In a large mixing bowl, combine beef, beans, stuffing mix, lime juice and pepper; mix lightly but thoroughly. Spread the mixture in a greased 12-inch pizza pan. Bake for 15 minutes or until the beef is thoroughly cooked. Sprinkle with pepper cheese and continue to bake for 2-3 minutes longer or until the cheese has melted. Sprinkle with onions and cut into 8 wedges. Garnish with lime wedges.

Florida Grilled Fish Roll-ups

"My wife and I have been making these for years and no matter how many we make, it never seems to be enough. These appetizers are guaranteed to disappear as fast as you can take them off the grill!"

Richard "Skip" Luckart—North Palm Beach

1 lb. sliced **Bacon**
1 lb. **Fish**, any kind,
  cut into bite-size pieces
1 medium **Onion**,
  sliced in 1-inch strips

1 can (8 oz.) sliced **Water Chestnuts**, drained
Toothpicks
Barbecue Sauce, for dipping

Cut bacon slices in half, separate and lay vertically on a flat surface. Starting at the end of each bacon strip, lay 1 piece of fish, 1 piece of onion and 1 slice of water chestnut. Roll up tightly and secure with a toothpick, making sure the toothpick goes completely through and securely holds opposite end of the bacon slice. Grill over medium heat for 5-6 minutes or until done; drain on paper towels. Serve hot, with barbecue sauce on the side.

Baked Cheese Papaya

This recipe is from the Historic Spanish Point: Cooking Then and Now cookbook.

Golf Coast Heritage Assoc., Inc—Historic Spanish Point, Osprey

1 carton (8 oz.) **Small-Curd Cottage Cheese**
1 package (8 oz.) **Cream Cheese**
1 tsp. **Curry Powder**
2 tbsp. **Mango Chutney**
2 tbsp. **Golden Raisins**

3 small **Papayas**, halved and seeded
3 tsp. **Sugar**
2 tsp. **Cinnamon**
2 tbsp. melted **Butter**

Pre-heat oven to 450 degrees. Cream cheeses together. Add curry, chutney and raisins. Fill the papaya halves with mixture. Place each half on a greased baking sheet. Sprinkle with sugar and cinnamon and drizzle with melted butter. Bake for 15 minutes.

Papaya & Red Onion Salsa

"When my husband and I bought our home, one of the first exotic fruit trees we planted was a papaya tree. This recipe is a family favorite. This salsa is especially good with grilled pork or grilled fish, or, serve with chips as an appetizer dip."

Liz Omler—Sarasota

1/2 ripe **Papaya**, peeled, seeded and chopped
2 tbsp. minced **Red Onion**
1/2 tbsp. minced **Jalapeño Pepper**
1 tbsp. finely chopped fresh **Cilantro**
2 tsp. fresh **Lime Juice**
1 tsp. **Maple Syrup**
Salt to taste

In a small mixing bowl, combine all ingredients, mix well. Cover and refrigerate until ready to serve.

Tangy Tangerine Salsa

"We came up with this recipe when wondering what to do with the abundance of tangerines from the 20-year-old tangerine tree in our yard. We experimented with salsas and finally came up with this one. Serve as a dip, or on the side with chicken."

Harald & Renate Zoschke—Suncoast Peppers, Inc., St. Petersburg

5-6 **Tangerines**, peeled, seeded and finely chopped
10 **Jalapeño Peppers**, seeded and finely chopped
1 small **White Onion**, finely chopped
1 tsp. **Ground Coriander**
2 tbsp. **Canola Oil**
2 tbsp. chopped fresh **Cilantro Leaves**
1-2 tsp. fresh grated **Ginger Root**

In a medium mixing bowl, combine all ingredients and mix gently. Allow to sit at room temperature for 30-45 minutes before serving or cover and refrigerate for later use. This salsa can be refrigerated for 2 days.

Mango-Champagne Fritters with Raspberry Sauce

"A favorite of our guests."

Erin and Bo Allen—Mango Inn Bed & Breakfast, Lake Worth

Batter.

2 cups **All-Purpose Flour**
1 **Egg Yolk**
Pinch of **Salt**
3 tbsp. **Powdered Sugar**
1 cup **Champagne**

2 **Egg Whites**
2 large ripe **Mango**, peeled, seeded and sliced thin
20 **Mint Leaves**

Combine and gently stir together the batter ingredients. Cover and let rest at room temperature for 1 hour. To prepare fritters, whip egg whites to stiff peak and then fold gently into batter. Press 1 or 2 mint leaves onto each mango slice and dip the mango into the batter. Deep fry in 350 degree oil until each fritter is golden brown. Remove and drain on paper towels. Serve with Raspberry Sauce for dipping.

Raspberry Sauce.

1/2 pint fresh **Raspberries**   **Sugar** to taste

Purée raspberries in blender, adding sugar to taste. Strain seeds from purée and set aside.

Lake Worth

Enjoy a concert at the Palm Beach Community College's Watson B. Duncan III Theater or visit their Museum of Art. Lake Osborne provides fine freshwater fishing or a multitude of saltwater species from one of Florida's longest municipally- owned Atlantic Ocean piers.

Mango Smoothie

"A great Florida refreshment!"

Erin and Bo Allen—Mango Inn Bed & Breakfast, Lake Worth

Pulp of 2 **Mangoes**
1 medium **Banana**, peeled and sliced
1 scoop **Vanilla Ice Cream**
2 tbsp. **Rum**
2 tbsp. **Sugar**
1 cup **Milk** or 1 cup **Orange Juice**

Place all ingredients in blender and blend until smooth. Pour over cracked ice in tall glasses.

Pensacola

It was here, in 1821, that Andrew Jackson completed the transaction by which Spain sold Florida to the U. S. Naval Air Station is an important part of this city and home to the Blue Angels precision flying team. Pensacola Beach has 20 miles of sugar-like sand.

Holiday Punch

"Whenever possible, I use fresh orange juice in this punch."

Margaret Friedling—St. Petersburg

2 packages (6 oz. ea.) **Cranberry Jell-0®**
2 cups **Hot Water**
1 can (6 oz.) frozen **Orange Juice Concentrate**
1 can (6 oz.) frozen **Lemonade Concentrate**
2 quarts **Cranberry Juice**
1 bottle (2 liter) **Lemon-Lime Soda** or **Ginger Ale**
Lemon Slices
Maraschino Cherries, halved

In a punch bowl, dissolve Jell-O in hot water. Stir in the concentrates and the cranberry juice and refrigerate overnight. Just before serving, pour in the ginger ale. Float lemon slices topped with halved cherries.

Christmas Punch

"A friend gave this recipe to me when I was first married 46 years ago. It is a favorite at Christmas, but can be used all year long. Be sure that each serving has a bit of the fruit in it."

Eleanor Harness—Sebring

1 cup **Gin**
1 cup **Whiskey**
1 cup **Rum**
1 large can (20 oz.) **Pineapple Tidbits**
1 large jar (10 oz.) **Maraschino Cherries**
1 can (12 oz.) frozen **Orange Juice Concentrate**
1/4 cup fresh **Lemon Juice**
Lemon-Lime Soda

In a punch bowl, mix all the ingredients together and refrigerate for several hours. When ready to serve, add soda to taste.

Sebring

Home to the Sebring International Race-way and, to the west, Highlands Hammock State Park, an area of more than 9,000 acres of wilderness, lush vegetation, jungle and swamp. Oak trees here range in age from 400 to nearly 1, 000 years old!

Syllabub

Marilyn & Robert Rice—Panama City

1/2 cup **Sugar**
Juice of 1 **Lemon**
4 tbsp. **Sherry**

1 tbsp. **Brandy**
1/2 pint **Whipping Cream**
Maraschino Cherry

Mix sugar, lemon juice and sherry. Stir until sugar is dissolved; blend in brandy. Whip the cream until firm and then gently blend with the sugar mixture. Pour into tall slender glasses. Chill until the cream and wine separate, about one hour. Top with a cherry. Serves 4-6.

Breakfast & Brunch

Banana Bread French Toast

"This is an unusual but delicious breakfast or brunch dish."

Annette Rawlings—Coconut Grove Bed & Breakfast Services,
Coconut Grove

1 cup **Sugar**
1/4 lb. **Unsalted Butter**, softened
4 **Eggs**
1 1/2 cups **All-Purpose Flour**
1 tsp. **Baking Soda**
1 tsp. **Salt**

1 cup mashed **Bananas**
1/2 cup **Sour Cream**
1 tsp. **Vanilla**
Oil, for frying
Powdered Sugar

Pre-heat oven to 350 degrees. In a bowl, cream sugar and butter together until light and fluffy. Add 2 eggs and blend well with a mixer. In another bowl, combine flour, baking soda and salt; add to creamed mixture and blend well. Stir in banana, sour cream and vanilla. Pour batter into a buttered 8 x 5 loaf pan. Bake for 1 hour. Remove bread, allow to cool slightly, then slice into 12 slices. Beat remaining eggs and dip bread slices to coat. Place slices on hot, oiled griddle and cook until golden brown on both sides. Sprinkle with powdered sugar.

Ham-Tomato Quiche

"Years ago a friend gave a going-away luncheon and served quiche. That was my first taste of a quiche and I developed an interest in trying different types of this delicious entreé. The following recipe is one of the results."

Cavelle Pawlock—Meadow Marsh Bed & Breakfast, Orlando

3 **Eggs**
1 can (12oz.) **Evaporated Milk**
1 tsp. **Garlic Powder**
1/4 tsp. **White Pepper**
1 tbsp. **Parsley**

6 slices cooked **Ham**, chopped
2 **Tomatoes**, chopped
1 (9-inch) baked **Pie Shell**
1 package (3 oz.) **Sharp Cheddar Cheese**, shredded

Pre-heat oven to 375 degrees. In a medium mixing bowl, beat eggs and milk together. Stir in garlic powder, pepper and parsley and mix well. Place ham and tomato in bottom of pie shell, pour egg mixture over the top and sprinkle with cheddar cheese. Bake for 25-35 minutes or until set in the middle and eggs are cooked. Serves 6.

Orlando

Nicknamed "The City Beautiful," this city, once a brawling frontier cattle town, is now considered one of the world's top tourist destinations. With Cape Canaveral 50 miles east and the 28,000-acre Walt Disney World complex just southwest, Orlando has become one of the fastest-growing metropolitan areas in the country. Here too can be found Universal Studios Florida, Jungleland, Splendid China (60 miniaturized replicas of landmarks—the Great Wall, Tibet's Potala Palace and the Stone Forest) and World of Orchids (thousands of exotic orchids in an enclosed tropical rainforest setting).

Tomato, Garlic Crouton & Pesto Omelet

"Omelets are as good at lunch and dinner as they are at breakfast. Here's one that celebrates the flavors of the Mediterranean and coastal living in every forkful. Serve with home fries for breakfast or lunch or with a serving of seafood for dinner."

Alice Morton—Florida Tomato Committee, Orlando

4 slices dense **White Bread** or
   Whole-Wheat Bread
1 tbsp. **Olive Oil**
1 clove **Garlic**, minced
2 large **Eggs**
1 tsp. **Water**
Pinch of **Salt**

1 tbsp. **Unsalted Butter**
1/4 to 1/3 cup grated
   Mozzarella Cheese
2 tbsp. **Pesto**
1/2 large **Tomato**, cut
   into bite-size pieces

Preheat oven to 300 degrees. Cut the bread into cubes, place in a mixing bowl and toss with olive oil and garlic. Spread cubes on a greased baking sheet, toast for 15-25 minutes until golden brown, then place on a plate to cool (This makes more croutons than you will need for one omelet. Save the leftovers for soup or salad). In a bowl, lightly beat eggs, water and stir with a fork in a circular motion. When the eggs start to set, spread out evenly across bottom of the pan and immediately turn heat to low. Cook for 3-5 seconds until the top layer of egg is almost entirely set, then sprinkle mozzarella cheese over the surface and dot with pesto. Scatter tomatoes and handful of croutons over half of the omelet, then fold the other half over the filled side. Cook until eggs are done. Serves 1.

Company Casserole

"This dish was originally prepared by a friend at a Mother's Day brunch over 20 years ago. It is now a staple in our crowd!"

Barbara Luckart—North Palm Beach

1 lb. medium or hot **Ground Sausage**
8 **Eggs**
4 cups **Milk**
12 oz. **Cheddar Cheese**, grated
1 tsp. **Salt**
Pepper to taste
1 tsp. **Dry Mustard**
1/3 cup finely chopped **Onion** (optional)
1/3 cup finely chopped **Green, Red** or **Yellow Bell Peppers** (optional)
8 slices **Bread**, cut into 1-inch cubes

In a large skillet, brown sausage, breaking into bite-size pieces, then drain. In a large mixing bowl, whip eggs, add milk, 2/3 of the cheddar cheese, salt, pepper, mustard, onion and peppers. Stir in bread cubes and sausage. Pour mixture into a greased 13 x 9 casserole dish, cover and refrigerate for 6 hours or overnight. Bake uncovered at 350 degrees for 45 minutes. Sprinkle remaining cheddar cheese over the top of casserole, return to the oven and bake for 10-15 minutes. Serve with side of salsa, fruit and Danish.

Fruit Butter

"This is great for muffins, biscuits, French toast or pancakes."

Teresa Campbell—Miami

1/2 cup **Butter**, softened
1/4 cup **Strawberry** or **Raspberry Preserves** or other mashed fresh fruit
1 tsp. **Lemon Juice**

Beat butter until fluffy, add fruit and lemon juice and stir until well-mixed.

Stuffed French Toast

"This is one of our guest's favorite Florida delights."

Cindy Montalto—Magnolia Plantation Bed & Breakfast Inn, Gainesville

3/4 cup softened **Cream Cheese**	1 cup fresh **Orange Juice**
2/3 cup **Orange Marmalade**	12 slices **Bread,** slightly
2 tbsp. **Honey**	frozen
5 **Eggs**	**Powdered Sugar**
	Orange Slices

In a small mixing bowl, combine cream cheese, marmalade and honey and gently stir until just combined. In a shallow bowl, whisk together eggs and orange juice. Spread cream cheese mixture on 6 slices of bread and top each with the remaining slices. Dip the "sandwiches" into egg mixture and place in a large, lightly-buttered skillet. Cook until browned on both sides. Cut into triangles and sprinkle with powdered sugar. Garnish with orange slices and serve immediately. Serves 6.

Gainesville

Above the University of Florida Auditorium is Century Tower, a 49-bell carillon that rings on quarter-hours. The 296,000-square foot O'Connell Center where fans enjoy Gator sports, has an air-supported roof. The Santa Fe Community College here is the only community college teaching zoo in the nation. Tom Petty of the "Heartbreakers" grew up here and the famous blues singer, Bo Diddley, is from nearby Hawthorne.

Super-Charged Breakfast

"Start your day out right with this Florida-style breakfast."

Nancy J. Pewonski—State of Florida Dept. of Citrus, Lakeland

1 medium **Grapefruit**
1 tbsp. **Honey**
1/4 tsp. **Cinnamon**
1/2 cup sliced **Strawberries, Raspberries** or **Blueberries**
1 small **Banana**, sliced
1/4 cup **Low-Fat Granola Cereal**
1/2 cup **Strawberry, Raspberry** or **Vanilla Nonfat Yogurt**
   (optional)

Peel the grapefruit, cut crosswise in half and separate out into sections. Stir honey and cinnamon together in small bowl. Divide fruit between two cereal bowls and drizzle with honey mixture. Top with granola and yogurt. Serves 2.

Did you Know?

There is a 9-foot, bronze underwater statue, "Christ of the Deep," which can be viewed by snorkel or scuba tours at John Pennecamp Coral Reef State at Key Largo.

Tropical Fruit Medley

A tropical delight for a tasty breakfast!

Florida Tropical Fruit Growers of South Florida—Homestead

1 **Papaya**, peeled, seeded and sliced
1 **Mango**, chopped
4 **Red Bananas**, sliced
1/2 lb. **Lychees**, peeled and seeded
Juice of 2 **Passion Fruit**
1 large **Annona**, pulped and strained with juice reserved

In a medium serving bowl, mix fruits together. Stir juice from passion fruit and annona together and pour over top of fruit mixture. Stir gently and serve. Serves 4.

Crepes & Eggs á la Mansion House

"This is great for a crowd, because you can make the crepes ahead, even freeze them if you choose."

Rose Marie Ray—Mansion House Bed & Breakfast, St. Petersburg

Crepes:

6 large **Eggs**
1 2/3 cups **Water**
1 2/3 cups **Milk**
6 tbsp. **Olive Oil**

2 cups **Wondra**® or other fine white **Flour**
1/2 tsp. **Salt**

Filling:

1 lb. **Mushrooms**, sliced
3 medium **Zucchini**, shredded
2 bags (24 oz. ea.) **Hash Brown Potatoes**
1 1/2 cups chopped **Ham**
48 **Eggs**
1 lb. **Gruyère** or **Swiss Cheese**, shredded

In a medium mixing bowl, beat eggs, then add water, milk and oil and whisk until blended. Gradually beat in the flour, adding drops of water to thin if necessary. Allow the mixture to set for 30 minutes or overnight. Heat an 8-inch skillet or crepe pan until hot, then add a drop of oil. Pour a small ladleful of batter into the pan, holding and tilting the pan so batter spreads out into a circle and covers the bottom. Brown lightly on one side, turn over and cook for 30 seconds. Slide crepe onto waxed paper and continue until batter is used, storing crepes between layers of waxed paper. In a skillet, add mushrooms and zucchini and sauté until tender. In another skillet, brown the potatoes and set aside. In a bowl, beat eggs and then pour into a nonstick skillet. Cook until almost done; stir in the vegetable mixture. Place a serving of potatoes in a single-serve baking dish, top with a single crepe, then spoon egg and vegetable mixture onto 1/2 of the crepe. Fold crepe and place with seam-side down. Top with ham and Gruyère cheese and broil for 1 minute or until cheese is melted. Serve with tomato slice and muffins. Serves 24.

Cheese Grits

"This recipe was handed down through several generations in my mother's family. I have eaten it for over 50 years. The original dish was a staple of early families in the Fort Myers area."

Lindsay Richards—Mount Dora Historic Inn, Mount Dora

4 cups **Water**	Dash fresh ground **Pepper**
1 cup **Grits***	1/2 cup **Milk**
1/4 tsp. minced **Garlic**	2 large **Eggs**, beaten
8 oz. **Cheddar Cheese**, diced	1/8 tsp. freshly grated
3/4 tsp. **Salt**	**Nutmeg**

Pre-heat oven to 350 degrees. In a microwavable container, bring water to boil in microwave. Add grits and cook for 10 minutes on 50% power, stirring twice to keep grits smooth. Add butter, garlic, cheddar cheese, salt and pepper. Stir until butter and cheese have dissolved. Allow grits to cool below 135 degrees, then fold in milk and eggs. Pour mixture into ramekins or a casserole dish and sprinkle with nutmeg. Bake for 50 minutes or until golden brown. Serves 8.

*For variety, substitute 1/2 cup each of yellow and white grits for the regular grits.

Classic Blueberry Muffins

Florida Blueberry Growers Association—Gainesville

2 cups **Flour**	2 **Eggs**
1/4 cup **Sugar**	3/4 cup **Milk**
3 tsp. **Baking Powder**	1/4 cup melted **Butter**
1/2 tsp. **Salt**	1 cup **Blueberries**

Pre-heat oven to 400 degrees. In a large bowl, mix the first four ingredients. In another bowl, whisk eggs, milk and butter together. Make a well in the dry ingredients and pour in egg mixture. Blend rapidly. Fold in blueberries. Spoon batter into 12 greased muffin cups and bake for 20-30 minutes or until golden brown.

Florida Blueberry Streusel Coffee Cake

Florida's blueberries are the first to ripen in North America and are large and flavorfully sweet. Blueberries contain vitamins A and C, are a good source of fiber, iron, and potassium, and are high in antioxidants.

Florida Blueberry Growers Association—Gainesville

Topping

1/2 cup packed **Brown Sugar**
3 tbsp. **Flour**
2 tsp. grated **Lemon Rind**
3 **Eggs**
2 cups **Flour**

1 tsp. **Baking Powder**
1 tsp. **Baking Soda**
1/2 tsp. **Salt**
1 cup **Sour Cream**
2 cups **Blueberries**

Pre-heat oven to 350 degrees. In a small bowl, combine all ingredients for the topping, except nuts, and stir until the mixture resembles fine crumbs. Stir in the nuts and set aside. In a large mixing bowl, cream butter until fluffy, add sugar and grated lemon rind and beat well. Add eggs, one at a time, beating well after each addition. In a bowl, combine dry ingredients. Add flour mixture to the creamed mixture alternately with the sour cream, blending well after each addition. Spread batter in a greased 13 x 9 baking pan. Sprinkle blueberries and then topping over the batter. Bake for 30-35 minutes. Serve warm.

Key West

This southernmost city in the continental U.S. once served as a base of operation against pirates. Just 90 miles southeast lies Cuba. Many visitors take the Conch train for a 10-mile tour of Key West.

Omelet Bake in Ramekins

"A favorite breakfast dish at our Inn"

Mike Breece—Sabal Palm House Bed & Breakfast Inn, Lake Worth

1 tbsp. **Butter**
Parmesan Cheese, for dusting
3 tbsp. **Extra-Virgin Oil**
1 medium **Onion**, diced
2 heads **Broccoli Florets**, chopped
1 large clove **Garlic,** minced
1/2 lb. **Smoked Ham**, diced
1 cup packed shredded **Gruyère Cheese**
12 **Eggs,** set at room temperature for 1 hour
1/2 cup **Milk**
Pinch of **Nutmeg**
Salt and **Pepper** to taste

Preheat oven to 350 degrees. Butter 4 ramekins and dust with the parmesan cheese. In a large skillet, heat oil, add onion and broccoli and sauté until onion is translucent. Add garlic and sauté for 1 minute, then stir in ham and cook until warmed through. Pour onion mixture equally into the ramekins and top with Gruyère cheese. In a medium mixing bowl, whisk eggs, milk, nutmeg, salt and pepper together and pour into the ramekins to just below the rim. Bake for 30 minutes or until top is browned and eggs are just cooked. Serve immediately.

Did you Know?

Legends of a fountain of youth brought the Spanish explorer Juan Ponce de León to the Florida region in 1513. He claimed the region for Spain and named it Florida because of the many flowers he saw there. The word Florida in Spanish means "full of flowers."

Soups, Stews, Chowders & Salads

Spanish Bean Soup

"This is a favorite recipe from Clara Mier, a descendant of one of the earliest families to settle in Florida."

Clementine Lowry Powers—St. Augustine

1 lb. **Garbanzo Beans**
1 **Soup Bone**
1 1/2 quarts **Water**
Salt and **Pepper** to taste
1/4 lb. **White Bacon** (Salt Pork)

1 large **Onion**, chopped
4 medium **Potatoes**, sliced
Pinch of **Saffron**
1 **Chorizo Sausage**, cut
  into thin slices

Sort beans, cover with water and soak overnight. Drain beans and place in a soup pot. Add soup bone and 1 1/2 quarts water; cook on low for 1 hour. Add salt and pepper. In a small skillet, fry bacon, remove from skillet, allow to cool and then crumble. Heat bacon drippings, add onion and sauté until translucent. Add onions, potatoes and saffron to beans and cook until potatoes are tender. Add sausage and stir well.=

Cioppino

"Cioppino is a seafood stew made with a tomato-based broth. It was originally created by Mediterranean fishermen. This version is simple and is easily adaptable to your favorite seafood. Serve with good bread and a glass of white wine."

Alice Morton—Florida Tomato Committee, Orlando

1/3 cup **Olive Oil**
2 large **Onions,** halved and thinly sliced
1 large **Green Bell Pepper,** chopped
2 cloves **Garlic,** minced
3 1/2 cups **Tomatoes,** cored, seeded and chopped
1 cup **Dry White Wine**
2 tbsp. **Tomato Paste**
1 **Bay Leaf**
1 tsp. fresh **Thyme** or 1/2 tsp. dried **Thyme**
1/4 tsp. **Salt**
1 can (6.5 oz.) **Clams,** chopped
1 1/2 lbs. **Cod, Haddock** or other boneless **Fish Fillets,** cut into
    2-inch pieces
1/2 lb. **Bay** or **Sea Scallops**
1 tbsp. chopped fresh **Basil** or 1 tsp. dried **Basil**
Salt and freshly ground **Black Pepper** to taste

In a large enameled soup pot or Dutch oven, warm olive oil over medium heat. Stir in onions and bell pepper and sauté, stirring occasionally, for 7 minutes. Add garlic and cook for 1 minute, then stir in tomatoes, wine, tomato paste, bay leaf, thyme and salt. Bring mixture to a simmer and cook, partially covered, for 10 minutes. Add clams, clam juice and fish, then cover and simmer for 5 minutes. Stir in scallops and basil, cover and simmer for 4-8 minutes or until scallops are done. Salt and pepper to taste. Remove bay leaf and serve while hot. Serves 4-6.

Did You Know?

Lake Okeechobee is the largest lake in the Southern United States. Okeechobee is a Seminole Indian word that means "plenty big water."

St. Augustine Minorcan Clam Chowder

"Clara Mier, the descendant of a family that came to Florida in the 1600's from Minorca, created this recipe for her El Patio restaurant."

Clementine Lowry Powers—St. Augustine

1/2 lb. **White Bacon** (Salt Pork), cubed
1 clove **Garlic**
2 large **Onions**, diced
1 large **Green Bell Pepper**, chopped
Salt and **Pepper** to taste
1 tsp. dried **Leaf Thyme**
1 can (28 oz.) **Whole Tomatoes**, chopped
2 cups **Hot Water**
1 quart fresh **Clams**, ground
1 **Hot Pepper**, seeded and diced

In a large heavy skillet, fry bacon until well done, remove from skillet and set aside. Add garlic, onion and bell pepper to bacon drippings and sauté until light brown. Add salt, pepper and thyme. Reduce heat, stir in tomatoes and simmer for 1 hour, adding a small amount of water if needed to keep from browning. Pour mixture into a large soup pot. Add hot water, clams and bacon. Cover and simmer until clams are cooked. Add hot pepper and stir.

Lemony Chicken-Rice Soup

4 cans (10.5 oz. ea.) **Chicken Broth**
1/4 cup uncooked **Rice**
2 **Eggs**
3 tbsp. fresh **Lemon Juice**
1/2 tsp. grated **Lemon Peel**
1 **Lemon**, sliced thin

In a saucepan, combine chicken broth and rice, cover and simmer until rice is tender. Place eggs and lemon juice in a bowl and whisk until fluffy. Pour two cups of hot broth mixture very slowly into egg mixture. Return egg mixture to saucepan and stir in lemon peel. Reheat, but do not boil. When serving, float lemon slices in each bowl.

Creamy Fresh Corn & Potato Chowder

Florida Supersweet Corn Council, Tallahassee

3 tbsp. **Butter**
3/4 cup chopped **Onion**
3/4 cup diced **Ham**
3 ears fresh **Supersweet Corn**, shucked

2 tbsp. **Flour**
2 1/2 cups **Milk**
1 3/4 cups diced **Red** Potatoes

Place butter, onion and ham in a 2-quart microwaveable casserole dish. Cover with waxed paper and microwave on high (100% power) for 5 minutes. Using a sharp knife, cut kernels from each ear while standing it upright on the flat end; reserve cobs and corn. In a small bowl, combine flour and milk, then pour on top of ham mixture. Add potatoes and reserved corn cob. Cover with waxed paper and microwave on high for 20 minutes, stirring after 10 minutes, until the soup is thickened and potatoes are tender. Discard cobs; stir in corn and cook for 5 minutes or until tender. Serves 4.

Miami-Miami Beach

Julia Tuttle, a Florida pioneer, convinced Henry Flagler to extend his Florida East Coast Railroad down to present-day Miami. The expansion was completed in 1896. The Miami metropolitan area has become one of the nations' most popular resort areas. Visit the Latin district of Little Havana on Calle Ocho or Vizcaya Museum and Gardens, a 10-acre villa built by James Deering. See cruise ships at the Port of Miam, said to handle more cruise passengers than any other in the world, or simply enjoy the many stretches of white sandy beaches to be found here.

Hendrix Farms Red Pepper Soup

"We love serving this delightful soup."

Charlotte Hendrix—C. W. Hendrix Farms, Boca Raton

1 tbsp. **Butter**
1 tbsp. **Olive Oil**
6 medium **Red** or **Yellow Bell Peppers**, seeded and cut into 1-inch pieces
1 large **Onion**, cut into 1-inch pieces
1 medium **Potato**, cut into 1-inch pieces
1 clove **Garlic**, minced
1 **Bay Leaf**
6 cups **Chicken Broth**
1 cup **Buttermilk**
1/2 cup shredded **Parmesan Cheese**

In a large saucepan, heat butter and oil; add peppers, onion, potato and garlic. Cover and cook on medium heat for 10 minutes or until onions are tender, stirring occasionally. Add bay leaf and broth, bring to a boil, then reduce heat and cover and simmer for 1 hour. Remove bay leaf, pour soup, 2 cups at a time, into a blender and blend until smooth. Strain soup, pour back into the pot and reheat. Serve, topped with parmesan cheese.

Citrus Tomato Soup

"Florida has always been know for its citrus products, so I experimented with lemon juice and orange rind to add 'tang" to this easy-to-prepare soup."

Cavelle Pawlack—Meadow Marsh Bed & Breakfast, Orlando

2 tbsp **Butter**
1 small **Onion**, chopped
1/2 cup chopped **Celery**
1 can (10.5 oz.) **Tomato Soup**
1 soup can **Water**
1/8 tsp. **White Pepper**
1 tbsp. **Lemon Juice**
1 tsp. grated **Orange Rind**
1 tsp. minced fresh **Parsley**
Whipped Cream
Parsley Flakes

In a skillet, melt butter, add onion and celery and sauté until onion is translucent. In a large saucepan, combine onion mixture, tomato soup and water. Stir in pepper, lemon juice, orange rind, salt and parsley and simmer for 5-8 minutes. Garnish with whipped cream and parsley flakes.

Fruit Salad Dressing

From *Citrus Lovers Cook Book* published by Golden West Publishers.

1/2 cup **Sugar**	1/4 cup **Red Jelly**
1 cup **Water**	1/4 cup **Lemon Juice**

Boil sugar, water and jelly for five minutes. Cover and refrigerate. When ready to use, add lemon juice, mix well and toss with your favorite fruits cut to bit-size pieces.

Indian River Grapefruit Salad

"This salad was named for the delicious grapefruit grown in this area."

1 cup **Boiling Water**	1/2 cup diced **Celery**
1 package (3oz.) **Lime Gelatin**	1 cup **Cottage Cheese**
1/4 tsp. ground **Ginger**	1/2 cup chopped **Pecans**
1 cup **Grapefruit Juice**	**Salad Greens**
1 cup **Grapefruit Sections,**	
membranes removed	

In a bowl, dissolve gelatin in boiling water, add ginger and grapefruit juice. Chill mixture until it starts to set, then add grapefruit, celery, cottage cheese and pecans and stir gently. Pour into a 5-6 cup mold and chill until firm. Un-mold salad onto crisp salad greens and drizzle with **Honey-Lime Dressing**. Serve with extra dressing on the side.

Honey-Lime Dressing

1/2 tsp. grated **Lime Rind**	1/2 tsp. **Paprika**
1/3 cup **Honey**	1/2 tsp. **Dry Mustard**
1/2 tsp. **Salt**	3/4 cup **Salad Oil**

In a blender, combine all ingredients, blend for 1 minute until smooth. Cover and refrigerate.

Did You Know?

St. Augustine is the nation's oldest continuously-inhabited white settlement. It was established by Spanish smuggler Pedro Menéndez de Avilés in 1565.

Joe's Vinaigrette

"This flavorful salad dressing is a favorite."

André Bienvenu—Joe's Stone Crab, Miami Beach

1/4 cup chopped **Sweet Onion**
3 tbsp. minced fresh **Parsley**
2 tbsp. chopped **Pimento**
1 hard boiled **Egg**, chopped
2 tbsp. minced fresh **Chives**
1 1/2 tsp. **Sugar**

1 tsp. **Salt**
1/2 tsp. **Cayenne**
1/2 cup drained **Capers**
1/3 cup **Cider Vinegar**
3/4 cup **Olive Oil**

In a bowl, whisk together all of the ingredients. Cover and store in refrigerator for at least 4 hours. Serve over chilled salad greens and vegetables of choice.

Grandmother Clifford's Frozen Fruit Salad

"My grandmother was well-known for this salad and it was delightful. She was one of the first in our family to have a refrigerator that would freeze or mold salads."

Betty Canaday—Melrose

1 cup chopped **Apricots**
1 jar (6oz.) **Maraschino Cherries**, sliced
1 cup **Mandarin Oranges**
1 cup chopped **Pears**
1 can (20 oz.) crushed **Pineapple**
2 **Bananas**, sliced
2 **Eggs**, beaten
4 tbsp. **Vinegar**
4 tbsp. **Sugar**
1 carton (16oz.) frozen **Whipped Topping**
1 jar (7oz.) **Marshmallow Cream**
1 cup chopped **Pecans**
Strawberries for garnish

Drain the first five fruits and set aside. In a heavy saucepan, combine eggs, vinegar and sugar and cook until thick, stirring constantly. Remove from the heat and allow to cool. Fold whipped topping and marshmallow cream into the egg mixture, then add fruit and pecans and mix well. Pour into individual molds and freeze for 24 hours. When serving, garnish with strawberries.

Frozen Orange Treats

From *Citrus Lovers Cook Book,* published by Golden West Publishers

Freeze oranges. When ready to use, remove from freezer and thaw, just until a hole a little larger that a soda straw can be cut from the peel. Massage and squeeze the oranges with hands to soften. Insert straw and give to children to provide a cool and healthy refreshment.

Fresh Spinach & Grapefruit Salad

Nancy J. Pewonski—State of Florida Dept. of Citurs, Lakeland

1 package (10 oz.) **Spinach Leaves**, washed, stemmed and torn
   into pieces
2 medium **Grapefruit**, peeled, cut crosswise and sectioned into
   pieces
1 **Red Bell Pepper**, cut into short, thin strips
1/2 cup sliced **Green Onion**
1/2 cup light **Honey-Dijon** or **Italian Salad Dressing**
1/4 cup low-fat **Bacon Bits**
1/2 cup fat-free **Seasoned Croutons**

In a large bowl, combine spinach, grapefruit, red pepper and onion. Add
dressing and toss well. Transfer salad to four serving plates and sprinkle
with bacon bits and croutons. Serves 4.

Did You Know?

*Gatorade was named for the University of Florida Gators where it
was first developed.*

The Florida Power Garden Salad

"This salad is designed for health and energy. I use as many organic fruits and vegetables as I can because they are higher in nutrition."

Barbara Passariello—Back to Basics Nutrition, Inc., Pompano Beach

1/2 head **Romaine Lettuce**, torn into pieces
2 cups fresh **Spinach Leaves**, torn into pieces
1/2 **Yellow Crookneck Squash**, diced
1 **Carrot**, diced
1/2 cup diced **Red Cabbage**
2 large **Radishes**, sliced
1/4 cup sliced **Red Onion**
2 **Green Onions**, chopped
1/2 **Red Delicious Apple**, chopped
1/4 **Green Bell Pepper**, chopped
1 stalk **Celery**, diced
1/4 cup **Alfalfa Sprouts**
1/2 cup frozen **Peas**, thawed
1/4 cup **Raisins**
1/4 cup **Feta Cheese**

In a large salad bowl, combine all the ingredients and toss well. Cover and chill before serving. Serve with salad dressing of choice. Serves 4-5.

Tallahassee

The Florida State Capital since 1845
The Oldest building is the Columns (1830)
Built by William "Money" Williams

Alfred B. Maclay State Gardens is a park that features the Maclay house and gardens that include azaleas, camellias and Oriental magnolias

Tallahassee Museum of History and Natural Science—52 acres of woodlands, cypress swamps and old fields

Kim's Cranberry Salad

"This has been a family favorite for years!"

2 **Red Apples**, pared
2 cups **Cranberries**
2 packages **Unflavored Gelatin**
1/2 cup **Water**
2 **Oranges**

1 cup **Sugar**
1/2 cup **Pecans**
1 can (8 oz.) crushed
   Pineapple, drained
   (reserve juice)
Lettuce

Place apples and cranberries in a blender and chop. Stir in sugar and set aside. Dissolve gelatin in water and set aside. Squeeze oranges to make 1 cup of juice, if necessary. Combine all ingredients and then cover and refrigerate until ready to serve. Serve on a bed of lettuce.

Main Dishes

Crab & Cheese Pie

"This is a great seafood pie recipe. When you live in Florida, you can always get crabmeat."

Lillian Madden—Williston

1 cup shredded **Swiss Cheese**
1 (9-inch) unbaked **Pie Shell**
1 cup **Crabmeat**
2 **Green Onions**, chopped
1 cup **Light Cream**
3 **Eggs**, beaten

1/2 tsp. grated **Lemon Rind**
1/4 tsp. **Dry Mustard**
1/2 tsp. **Salt**
1/4 cup sliced **Almonds**
Parsley

Pre-heat oven to 325 degrees. Sprinkle Swiss cheese in the bottom of the pie shell and follow with crabmeat and onion. In a bowl, combine cream, eggs, lemon rind, mustard and salt; mix well. Pour egg mixture over onion and crabmeat and sprinkle almonds on the top. Bake for 1 hour. Allow to set for 10 minutes before slicing. Garnish with parsley, if desired. Serves 6-8.

Sautéed Gulf Coast Grouper

"A waiter at The Colony brought Chef John some very juicy, sweetly tart tangelos. Chef John created this recipe especially with the tangelos in mind, but fresh oranges can be used since different varieties are available year-round. Tailor this recipe with your favorite, according to the season."

Liza Kubik—The Colony Restaurants, Longboat Key

Florida Orange Coulis

1 quart **Florida Orange Juice**
1/2 cup packed **Brown Sugar**

1/2 cup **Whole Butter**

Vegetable Ratatouille

Extra Virgin Olive Oil,
  as needed for sautéing
1/2 cup diced **Eggplant**
1/2 cup diced **Zucchini**
1/2 cup diced **Yellow Squash**

Roasted Garlic Purée to taste
Kosher Salt to taste
Freshly ground **Black Pepper**
  to taste
1/2 cup diced **Tomatoes**

Grouper.

4 (7 oz. ea.) fresh **Grouper Fillets**
Kosher Salt to taste
Freshly ground **Black Pepper** to taste
Extra Virgin Olive Oil, as needed for sautéing
1 cup **White Wine**
Vegetable Oil, for deep drying
2 medium **Potatoes**, julienne or mandoline into matchsticks
Fresh **Orange** segments, for garnish

To prepare Orange Coulis, heat orange juice in a medium saucepan and cook until reduced by half. Add brown sugar, adjusting sweetness to taste, then stir in butter. Consistency should be slightly thick. To prepare Ratatouille, in a medium skillet, heat oil and sauté eggplant, zucchini and yellow squash until tender. Season mixture with garlic purée, salt and pepper, then add the tomatoes and toss. Remove from heat and set aside. Preheat oven to 375 degrees. Season the fish fillets and pan-sear in oil in a hot skillet for 1 minute on one side. Turn over, add wine and shake to loosen fillets from pan. Finish baking in the oven for approximately 8 minutes or until cooked to opaque. Using mandoline slicer, julienne the potatoes and deep-fry in hot oil until crisp; set aside. Arrange portion of Ratatouille vegetables in the center of each plate. Place the cooked fish around Ratatouille. Ladle a small amount of Orange Coulis over the fish. Garnish with crispy fried potato matchsticks and orange segments.

Tangelos

A tangelo is any citrus fruit that results from cross-pollination between tangerine and pomelo (the old name for grapefruit) trees.

Savory Chuck Steaks

"A quick and easy Florida-style grilled steak."

Polly Golden—Florida Beef Council, Kissimmee

1/4 cup **Steak Sauce**	1/4 tsp. ground **Red Pepper**
2 tbsp. **Brown Sugar**	4 boneless beef **Chuck Eye**
2 tbsp. fresh **Lime Juice**	**Steaks**, cut 1-inch thick

In a small bowl, combine steak sauce, brown sugar, lime juice and pepper; reserve 2 tablespoons of marinade. Place steaks in a plastic bag, add remaining marinade and turn bag to coat meat well. Close bag securely and marinate for 10 minutes. Pour off marinade and place steaks on a grill over medium coals. Grill for 14-20 minutes (for rare to medium), turning once. Brush with reserved marinade during the last 2 minutes of cooking. Season with salt, if desired. **Red Onion** wedges and **Zucchini** slices can be brushed with the marinade and grilled along with the steaks.

Drunken Shrimp

"My husband and I are 'snowbirds,' spending the winter months in Florida. We serve this dish to our northern friends when they come down and visit."

Sylvia Cox Barr—Destin

1 lb. (18-20) medium **Shrimp**	2 tbsp. **Shallots** or **Green**
1/4 cup freshly squeezed	**Onions**
Lime Juice	1/4 cup **Tequila**
Salt and **Pepper** to taste	3/4 cup **Half and Half**
2 1/2 tbsp. Butter	1 ripe **Avocado**
	2 tbsp. chopped fresh **Cilantro**

Shell and devein shrimp. Butterfly by splitting partially down the back. In a bowl, combine lime juice, salt and pepper. Add shrimp, turning to cover on all sides; let set for 10-15 minutes; drain. Peel and slice avocado. In a medium skillet, heat butter, add shrimp and cook 2-3 minutes, stirring constantly. Add shallots and cook for 30 seconds, continuing to stir while cooking. Carefully add tequila to avoid flare-up, then add half and cook over high heat for 1 minute. Stir in lime juice mixture and the avocado and continue to cook for 1 minute. With a slotted spoon, transfer shrimp and avocado to serving dish. Bring sauce to a full boil and cook for 2-3 minutes, then stir in cilantro. Spoon sauce over shrimp and avocado mixture. Serve with rice. Serves 4.

At Daytona International Speedway, the Daytona 500 automobile race is held each February. The Speedway features eight weekends of stock car and motorcycle racing each year.

Pompano Bake in Sour Cream Sauce

"This recipe is of Russian origin. Pampano, Red Snapper and Yellowtail are often caught in Florida waters and are perfect for this dish."

Drollene . Brown—A+ Writing, Morriston

2 lbs. **Pompano**, boned and skinned	**Salt** and **Pepper** to taste
2 tbsp. **Flour**	1/2 cup grated **Cheddar Cheese**
1/2 stick **Butter**	**Sour Cream Sauce**
2 hard boiled **Eggs**, peeled and sliced	(prepare ahead)

Preheat oven to 350 degrees. Cut fish fillets into 4 portions and roll in flour. In a large skillet, melt 1/4 stick of butter and sauté fillets for 3-4 minutes on both sides. Place fillets in a buttered baking dish and layer egg slices on top. In the large skillet, sauté mushrooms for 4-5 minutes. Spoon mushrooms on top of eggs. In the same skillet, melt remaining butter, add potatoes and cook until tender. Arrange potatoes around the fish, eggs and mushrooms. Sprinkle with salt and pepper. Pour Sour Cream Sauce over casserole, then sprinkle top with cheddar cheese. Bake for 20-25 minutes.

Sour Cream Sauce

1/2 stick **Butter**	1 cup **Sour Cream**
2 tbsp. **Flour**	**Salt** to taste
1 cup **Meat** or **Vegetable Stock**, warmed	

In a medium saucepan, melt butter, then add flour and blend until smooth. Gradually add warmed stock, stirring to blend, then add sour cream and blend thoroughly. Add salt as desired and simmer gently for 5-10 minutes.

Citrus Fish Fillets à la Florida

"This recipe was handed down from my grandmother and has become a family favorite. We catch and fillet our own fish, using whatever fish is in season, for this recipe."

Alice Silva—St. Augustine

5 cups **Water**
5 **Chicken Bouillon Cubes**
2 cups **Uncle Ben's® Converted Rice**
1/4 cup **Flour**
Pinch of **Oregano**

1/2 tsp. **Garlic-Parsley Salt**
4 **Fish Fillets**, skinned
1/4 cup **Butter**
1 **Orange, Tangerine** or small **Grapefruit**, sliced
1 **Lemon**, sliced

In a large pan, bring water to a boil, add bouillon cubes, lower heat, add rice and cook until rice is tender. In a shallow bowl, combine flour, oregano and garlic-parsley salt. Dredge fish fillets in seasoning until well coated. In a large, nonstick frying pan, melt butter and add fillets. Cook for approximately 5 minutes per side or until golden brown. On a serving platter, spread a bed of rice, place the fillets on top and garnish with sliced citrus. Squeeze lemon slices over fish. Serves 4.

The Everglades & Everglades National Park

This is the largest remaining subtropical wilderness in the nation. Covering 2,746 square miles in the southern part of Florida, the Everglades stretch southward from Lake Okeechobee in a sweep about 40 miles wide and 100 miles long and merge into saltwater marshes and mangrove swamps near the Bay of Florida and the Gulf of Mexico. In 1947, the southwestern part of the region became the Everglades National Park.

Spicy Alligator Gumbo

A favorite Florida recipe from Alligator Bob's Gourmet Alligator Cookbook.

Robert N. Young—Alligator Bob's, Plant City

1 lb. uncooked **Alligator Nuggets**
2 tbsp. **Vegetable Oil**
2 tbsp. **All-Purpose Flour**
2 cans (14.5 oz. ea.) stewed **Tomatoes, Cajun-style**
2 cans (8 oz. ea.) **Clam Juice**
2 cups sliced fresh or frozen **Okra**
2 tsp. dried **Thyme**
Hot Pepper Sauce to taste
Salt and **Pepper** to taste

Cut up alligator nuggets into small pieces. In a medium saucepan, heat oil, then add flour and stir until roux turns deep brown. Add tomatoes and break into pieces with the back of a spoon. Add clam juice, okra, thyme and alligator nuggets and stir until well-blended. Reduce heat to medium-low, cover and simmer until alligator is tender. Uncover and cook until broth thickens slightly. Add hot pepper sauce and season with salt and pepper to taste. Serve over white rice or noodles. Serves 6.

Fort Myers

Fort Myers was once the winter home to two of America's foremost 20th century industrialists, Thomas Edison and Henry Ford. Edison perfected inventions such as the incandescent light bulb, phonograph, storage battery and the motion picture camera at his winter home, "Seminole Lodge." A banyan tree in Edison's garden is the largest of its kind in Florida. Ford's home, "Mangoes," has been restored and furnished in 1920's style. Ford was the world's first billionaire.

Larry Joe's Wild Hog Stew

"This dish was given to me by rancher friends who were born and raised in the Sebring area."

Fran Bennett—Sebring

2 lbs. **Wild Hog**, chunked
4 medium **Potatoes**, chopped
1 can (14.5 oz.) **Green Beans**
1 can (15.25 oz.) **Corn**

1/2 cup **Water**
1 can (15 oz.) **Carrots**
3 tbsp. **Everglades® Seasoning**
(or any hot and spicy
seasoning)

Combine all ingredients in a large crock pot and cook on low for approximately 5 hours or until meat is done.

Chicken Tacos

"I had a girlfriend from Mexico who used chicken when making tacos as they did not have beef were they lived. My children loved tacos made this way!"

Lillian Madden—Williston

1 can (19 oz.) **Green Chile Sauce**
12 hard **Taco Shells**
1 **Chicken**, boiled, de-boned and diced
1 head **Lettuce**, finely shredded
1 **Tomato**, diced
1/4 lb. **Cheddar Cheese**, shredded
1 carton (8 oz.) **Sour Cream**

In a medium saucepan, warm green chile sauce. Fill taco shells with chicken and spoon sauce over the meat. Top with lettuce, tomato, cheese and sour cream as desired. Serves 5-6.

Sautéed Chicken with Grapefruit Sauce

This recipe includes Florida's fresh vegetables and especially, Florida grapefruit!

2 cups quick-cooking **Brown Rice**
2 cups fresh **Vegetables***, chopped
4 (4 oz.) skinless, boneless **Chicken Breast Halves**
1 tsp. dried **Rosemary,** crushed
1/2 tsp. **Salt**
1/4 tsp. freshly ground **Black Pepper**
1 tbsp. **Olive Oil**
1/2 cup chopped **Onion**
2 cloves **Garlic**, minced
1/2 cup **Chicken Broth**
1 tbsp. **Cornstarch**
1/4 cup **Orange Marmalade**
2 medium **Florida Grapefruit**, sectioned

Prepare rice according to package directions, stirring in vegetables during last 5 minutes of cooking. Sprinkle chicken with rosemary, salt and pepper. Heat oil in a large skillet over medium heat. Add chicken, onion and garlic; cook 5 minutes or until chicken is cooked through. Transfer chicken to a plate; set aside. Combine broth and cornstarch: mix well. Add to skillet: cook and stir until sauce thickens. Stir in marmalade: add grapefruit and mix well. Return chicken to skillet, turning to coat with sauce. Serve chicken and grapefruit sauce over rice.

*Include fresh vegetables such as broccoli florets, shredded carrots, diced bell peppers and chopped zucchini.

Did You Know?

Florida produces about three-fourths of the United States citrus products.

Beef Enchilada Casserole

"This is a family favorite that we often take to get-togethers."

Alice Silva—St. Augustine

1 lb. **Ground Beef**
1 tsp. **Chili Powder**
1 tbsp. **Paprika**
3 tbsp. **Flour**
2 can (8 oz.) **Tomato Sauce**
1/4 cup **Water**

1 cup pitted **Black Olives**
8 **Corn Tortillas**
1 **Onion**, chopped
1 cup shredded **American**
   or **Cheddar Cheese**

Pre-heat oven to 350 degrees. In a large skillet, brown beef lightly then add salt, chili powder, paprika and flour. Mix well; add tomato sauce and water. Bring the mixture to a boil, stirring constantly. Stir in olives and simmer for 10 minutes. Spoon a thin layer of meat sauce into shallow baking dish. Layer with 4 corn tortillas, then add 1/2 of the remaining sauce. Sprinkle with 1/2 of the onion and cheese and repeat the layer. Bake for 20-30 minutes or until cheese melts.

Spicy Shrimp & Potato Skillet

"The shrimp in this recipe comes from Florida.
This is an excellent and unusual way to fix shrimp."

Shirley Booth—Burton's Sheds, Sebring

5-6 **Red Potatoes**, quartered
Old Bay Spice® to taste
Salt and **Pepper** to taste

1 lb. **Jumbo Shrimp**, cleaned
   and deveined
2 medium **Onions**, quartered

Place potatoes in a large deep skillet and cover with water. Cook until potatoes are tender. Add Old Bay and shrimp and cook shrimp until almost done. Add onions, more Old Bay, salt and pepper and cook until onions are tender. Serve in skillet with garlic bread on the side. Serves 4.

Barbara's Easy Linguini Marinara with Hummus

"I am a licensed nutritionist who lectures, teaches and writes a monthly nutrition column for a local paper. This is one of my 'healthy' favorites that I like to share."

Barbara Passarello—Back to Basics Nutrition, Inc., Pampano Beach

1/2 cup **Olive Oil**
1 large clove **Garlic,** diced
1/2 medium **Sweet Onion**, diced
1 jar (26-30 oz.) **Tomato Sauce**
1/2 tsp. **Oregano**
1 tbsp. dried **Basil Flakes**
2 **Bay Leaves**
1/2 -3/4 cup **Water**
1 package (12 oz.) **Linguini Noodles**
1 1/2 cups prepared **Hummus**
Pine Nuts, for garnish
Chopped fresh **Parsley**, for garnish

In a medium saucepan, heat oil, add garlic and onion and sauté until golden brown. Add tomato sauce, herbs and water, then cover and simmer for 20 minutes. While sauce is simmering, prepare pasta following instructions on package. Add hummus to sauce and simmer for 5 minutes longer; remove bay leaves. Drain pasta, stir in sauce and sprinkle with pine nuts and parsley.

Apalachicola National Forest

Encompassing 565,000 acres in northwestern Florida, this is the largest of Florida's three national forests. Its name is derived from a Hitchiti Indian word meaning "people on the other side." Approximately 10% of the nation's total oyster crop is cultivated in more than 6,000 acres of oyster beds in Apalachee Bay.

Cuban Chicken Pie

*"My mother-in-law received this recipe from one of her
Cuban friends and shared it with me."*

Lea Ann Baker—Miami

1 whole **Chicken**
Salt and **Pepper** to taste
1 medium **Onion**, quartered
2 **Bay Leaves**
3 tbsp. **Olive Oil**
1 **Green Bell Pepper**, chopped
1 **Onion**, diced
4 cloves **Garlic**, minced
1 small jar (4 oz.) **Pimentos,** drained and chopped
1/2 cup **Dry Sherry** or **White Wine**
1-2 cans (8 oz. ea.) **Tomato Sauce**
1/2 cup chopped **Green Olives**
1/2 cup **Raisins**
1/2 cup **Peas**
3 packages refrigerated **Croissant Rolls**
2 hard boiled **Eggs**, sliced

Pre-heat oven to 350 degrees. In a large pot, cover chicken with water, add salt, pepper, onion and 1 bay leaf. Bring water to a boil and cook the chicken until tender. Remove chicken, let cool, and debone and shred the meat. In a large skillet, heat oil, add bell pepper, onion and garlic and sauté until thickened. Add peas. Unroll the croissant dough and line two pie pans with enough to form bottom pie crusts, pinching seams together to seal; reserve enough to make top crusts. Divide chicken mixture evenly and spoon into pans, topping each with the egg slices. Place remaining croissant dough on top as a crust. Bake until golden brown.

Did You Know?

Fort Lauderdale, just north of Miami, is known as the Venice of America because the city has 185 miles of local waterways.

Pane Cotto

(Pah-nay cotto means "cooked bread" in Italian)

"This is an Old World Neapolitan peasant food."

Elsa Addario—Hot Tomatoe, Lighthouse Point

Oil
3 cloves **Garlic**, minced
1 lb. bulk **Italian Sweet Sausage**
1 large head **Escarole** or **Endive**
1/2 can (15 oz.) **Cannelini Beans**, drained
Stale Bread, broken into chunks
Salt and **Pepper** to taste

In a large skillet, add oil and sauté garlic until brown. Add sausage and cook thoroughly. Steam escarole until tender, add to sausage mixture and stir in beans. Simmer for 10 minutes. Toss in bread and add salt and pepper to taste.

Black-Eyed Pea Supper

This recipe is from the Historic Spanish Point: Cooking Then and Now cookbook.

Gulf Coast Heritage Association, Inc.—Osprey

1 package (16 oz.) **Black-Eyed Peas**
2 lbs. bulk **Pork Sausage**
1/2 cup chopped **Onions**
1 can (28 oz.) **Whole Tomatoes**
2 1/2 tbsp. finely chopped **Celery**
2 1/2 tbsp. **Chili Powder**
2 tsp. **Garlic Salt**
1/4 tsp. **Pepper**
2 tbsp. **Sugar**

Wash and pick over peas. Place in a large pot, cover with water and soak overnight. Brown sausage in a heavy skillet, stirring to crumble. Add onions and cook for 10 minutes. Drain. Drain peas and place in a large Dutch oven. Stir in sausage mixture and balance of ingredients. Bring to a boil and cook slowly for 1 1/2 hours.

Florida-Style Grouper Delite with Key Lime Butter Topping

"This is a special blend of fresh Florida fish and citrus for a truly Floridian dish."

Mark Campbell—Muckey Duck, Fort Meyers Beach

2 tsp. **White Wine**
2 tsp. **Lemon Juice**
2 (8 oz. ea.) **Grouper Fillets**
1 tbsp. **Butter**
1 clove **Garlic**, minced
Salt and **Pepper** to taste
1 tbsp. diced **Shallots**
1 tsp. fresh **Parsley**
4 oz. **Blue** or **Stone Crabmeat**

Combine white wine with lemon juice and season fish fillets with 1/2 of the mixture. Broil fillets at 350 degrees for 12 minutes. In a small skillet, heat butter and sauté remaining wine mixture, garlic, salt, pepper, shallots, parsley and crabmeat. Arrange fillets on a serving platter, place crab meat on top and cover with **Key Lime Butter Topping.**

Key Lime Butter Topping

1/2 cup **Heavy Cream**
1/8 cup **Key Lime Juice**
1/8 tsp. **Lemon Herb**
Dash of **White Pepper**
Dash of **Salt**
Dash of fresh **Parsley** or **Dill**
1/8 cup **White Wine**
1/8 cup **Cornstarch**
1/8 cup **Water**
1/2 lb. **Butter**, softened

In a medium saucepan, combine cream, Key lime juice, lemon herb, pepper, salt, parsley and wine and bring the mixture to a boil. Blend cornstarch and water until smooth, stir into cream mixture, add butter and continue to stir until smooth.

Seafood

Seafood Tips

Seafood tips and recipes in this section were provided by Bob Crawford, Commissioner—Florida Department of Aquaculture and Consumer Services, Tallahassee.

When Buying Seafood

When food shopping, purchase seafood last and keep it cold. Ask your grocer to pack seafood on ice for the trip home.

Storing Seafood

Store seafood in a leak-proof container for no more than two or three days at refrigerator temperatures (32-38°F), or three to ten months frozen.

Storing Oysters and Clams

Never store live (in the shell) oysters or clams in airtight containers. Refrigerate for no more that five days. Both will naturally open during storage. Tap the shell lightly. If they do not close, they are dead and must be discarded.

Prevent Cross-Contamination

Wash your hand before and after handling raw seafood. Do not drip seafood juices on counters, utensils or other foods, and thoroughly wash containers that held raw seafood before using them again.

When in Doubt, Throw it Out!

Never eat or even taste a food that you think might be spoiled.

Marinating Seafood

Always marinate seafood in the refrigerator.

Cooking Fresh Fish

In general, fish should be cooked for 10 minutes per inch at 400 to 450 degrees , turning the fish halfway through the total cooking time. If fish is cooked in a sauce or foil, add five minutes to the cooking time.

Cooking Frozen Fish

Double all suggested cooking times if cooking unthawed fish.

When is Fish Done?

Fish is done when the flesh becomes opaque and flakes easily at the thickest part.

Cooking Shrimp & Scallops

Shrimp and scallops become opaque and firm when fully cooked. One pound of medium shrimp should be boiled or steamed for three to five minutes. Scallops should be broiled for three to five minutes or fried until opaque.

Cooking Oysters & Clams

Oysters and clams are steamed or broiled until the shells pops open, fried in oil for three to four minutes at 375 degrees, or baked for 10 minutes at 450 degrees.

Stir-Frying with Seafood

Cook seafood separately. When balance of stir-fry ingredients are cooked to desired doneness, add in seafood only long enough to warm thoroughly.

Curried Stone Crab Claws with Hot Marmalade Soy Dip

2 1/2 lbs. frozen **Stone Crab Claws**
1/2 cup **Butter**, softened
1 tsp. **Curry Powder**

Crack and remove the outer shell of the crab claw, leaving meat attached to one side of the claw. Cream together butter and curry powder. Spread curry butter mixture over both sides of each claw and arrange them on a broiling pan. Broil about 3 inches from broiler unit for 6-8 minutes, turning once. Serve **Hot Marmalade Soy Dip** on the side. Serves 6.

Hot Marmalade Soy Dip

1/3 cup **Orange Marmalade**
1/4 cup **Lemon Juice**
1/4 cup **Soy Sauce**
1 clove **Garlic**, minced
1/8 tsp. **Ginger**
1 tsp. **Cornstarch**

Combine all ingredients in a small saucepan and mix well. Cook, stirring constantly, until clear and thickened.

Cheese-Crusted Amberjack

2 lbs. **Amberjack Fillets**
1/2 cup **Herb & Garlic Salad Dressing**
1/2 cup crushed **Corn Flakes**
1/2 cup shredded **Sharp Cheddar Cheese**
6 thin **Orange Slices**

Pre-heat oven to 45 degrees. Cut fish into serving-size portions. In a shallow baking dish, arrange fillets in single layer. Pour dressing over fish; cover and marinate in refrigerator for several hours, turning fish 3-4 times. In a small bowl, combine corn flakes and cheese and mix well. Roll fish in crumb mixture to coat. Arrange fish in lightly- oiled baking dish and sprinkle with remaining crumb mixture. Bake for 15 to 20 minutes or until fish flakes easily with fork. Garnish with orange slices. Serves 6.

Roasted Florida Clams

2-4 dozen **Clams**, in the shell   **Butter** or **Seafood Sauce**

Preheat oven to 350 degrees. Wash clams thoroughly under cold running water. Arrange on a lightly-oiled baking sheet on the middle oven rack. Roast clams for about 10 minutes or until clams open. Serve in the shells with butter or a favorite seafood sauce.

Baked Stuffed Lobster

2 (1 lb. ea.) frozen whole green/raw **Lobsters**, thawed
1 1/2 cups soft **Bread Crumbs**
1/2 cup grated **Cheddar Cheese**
2 tbsp. **Butter**, melted
1 tbsp. grated **Onion**
Paprika

Preheat oven to 400 degrees. Cut lobsters in half lengthwise; remove stomach and intestinal vein. Rinse with cold water and clean body cavity thoroughly. Combine bread crumbs, cheese, butter and onion. Stuff mixture into body cavity and spread over surface of the tail meat. Sprinkle with paprika. Arrange in a shallow baking dish and bake for 15 to 20 minutes or until lightly browned. Serves 2.

Grilled Florida Clams

2 to 4 dozen **Clams**, in the shell   **Butter** or **Seafood Sauce**

Wash clams thoroughly under cold running water and arrange on a grill about 4 inches from the hot coals. Roast for approximately 10 minutes or until clams open. Serve in the shells with melted butter or a favorite seafood sauce.

Seafood Feast

1/2 lb. **Scallops**, cooked
1/2 lb. **Shrimp**, cooked, peeled and deveined
1/2 lb. **Fish**, cooked and cubed
1 small **Onion**, sliced and separated into rings
1/2 cup small fresh **Mushrooms**
1 cup **Cherry Tomatoes**
1/4 cup **Lime Juice**
2 cloves **Garlic**, minced
1/8 tsp. **White Pepper**
2 cups **Low-Calorie Italian Salad Dressing**
Salad Greens

In a large mixing bowl, combine all ingredients, except salad greens, and mix thoroughly. Cover tightly and refrigerate for 8 hours. Drain and serve on a bed of greens. Serves 6.

Peppy Cocktail Sauce

1/2 cup **Ketchup**   1 tbsp. **Horseradish**
1/2 cup **Chili Sauce**   1/2 tsp. grated **Onion**
3 tbsp. **Lemon Juice**   1/4 tsp. **Salt**
1 tsp. **Worcestershire Sauce**   1/4 tsp. **Hot Pepper Sauce**

In a medium bowl, combine all ingredients and stir until thoroughly mixed. Chill and serve. Yields 1 1/2 cups.

Steamed Clams

2 dozen **Clams**, in the shell
1 cups **Dry Sherry**
1/2 cup chopped **Green Onions**

2 tsp. minced **Garlic**
2 tsp. fresh grated **Ginger**

Wash clams thoroughly under cold running water and set aside. In a large saucepan, combine all ingredients, except clams. Simmer on medium heat for 3 minutes; add clams and cover. When clams open, remove them to a large bowl. Simmer remaining liquid until it is reduced to 3/4 cup. Pour liquid over clams and serve. Serves 4.

Fort Lauderdale

This city, with its miles of beaches and waterways has become one of the most popular areas on the Gold Coast. Favorite events include the Las Olas Art Fair in January and February, where artists from all across the nation exhibit. The Seafood Festival in April is another favorite. Christmas brings the spectacular Winterfest Boat Parade. Decorated boats cruise from Port Everglades up the Intercoastal Waterway to Pompano Beach, and back again.

Broiled Scallops

1 1/2 lbs. **Scallops**
1/4 cup **Butter**, melted
3 tbsp. **Lime Juice**
1 tsp. minced **Garlic**

1/2 tsp. **Salt**
1/8 tsp. **White Pepper**
1/8 tsp. **Paprika**
2 tbsp. chopped fresh **Parsley**

Rinse scallops under cold running water; pat dry with paper towels. Arrange scallops on a lightly-oiled broiler pan. Combine butter, lime juice, garlic, salt, pepper and paprika. Brush scallops with seasoned butter. Broil about 3 inches under broiler unit for 3 to 4 minutes; turn. Brush other side of scallops with seasoned butter and broil for an additional 3-4 minutes. Garnish with parsley. Serves 6.

Vegetable Stuffed Catfish

6 pan-dressed **Catfish**　　　　6 slices **Bacon**, cut in thirds
2 tsp. **Salt**　　　　　　　　　　**Paprika**

Vegetable Stuffing:

1/3 cup **Butter**　　　　　　　2 cups soft **Bread Crumbs**
1 cup grated **Carrots**　　　　1 tbsp. **Lime Juice**
3/4 cup chopped **Celery**　　　1/2 tsp. **Salt**
1/2 cup chopped **Onions**

Preheat oven to 350 degrees. To prepare stuffing, melt butter in a medium saucepan, add vegetables and cook until tender, stirring occasionally. Add remaining ingredients for stuffing and mix lightly. Sprinkle fish with salt and stuff with vegetable stuffing. Arrange fish in a well-oiled 14 x 11 pan. Place 3 pieces of bacon on each fish, then sprinkle with paprika. Bake for 25-30 minutes. Turn on broiler, place fish 3 inches under broiler unit and broil for 2-3 minutes or until bacon is crisp. Serves 4.

Grilled Striped Bass

1/4 cup **Soy Sauce**　　　　　　2 tbsp. **Vegetable Oil**
2 tbsp. **Sugar**　　　　　　　　2 tbsp. **Sesame Seeds**
1 tbsp. finely minced **Garlic**　　2 lbs. **Striped Bass Fillets**,
1 tbsp. finely minced **Green**　　skin on
Onions

In a small bowl, combine soy sauce, sugar, garlic, onion and oil; set aside. In a small skillet, lightly brown sesame seeds over low heat, stirring constantly. Remove from heat and add to soy sauce mixture. Arrange fillets, skin side down, in a shallow baking dish. Pour soy sauce mixture over fish, cover and marinate in refrigerator for 30 minutes, turning once. Remove from marinade and arrange fish on a well-oiled grill, skin-side down, about 4-6 inches from hot coals. Discard marinade. Grill fish for 4-5 minutes or until fish flakes easily with a fork. Do not turn fish over or the fillets will fall apart. Serves 6.

Batter Fried Shark

2 lbs. **Shark Fillets**
1 cup **All-Purpose Flour**
1 tbsp. **Salt**
1 tsp. **Baking Powder**

1 cup **Water**
1 tbsp. **Vinegar**
Vegetable Oil

Cut fish into 1-inch cubes. In a bowl, combine flour, salt and baking powder. Slowly add water and vinegar and mix well. Dip fish cubes in batter and carefully drop into hot (425 degrees) oil. Cook 2-3 minutes or until golden brown. Drain on paper towels. Serves 6.

Broiled Swordfish

2 lbs. **Swordfish Steaks**

Marinade

1/4 cup **Vegetable Oil**
1/4 cup **Tarragon Vinegar**
1 tsp. **Salt**
1/4 tsp. **Paprika**

1 clove **Garlic**, sliced
1/8 tsp. **Cayenne**
Paprika
Chopped fresh **Parsley**

Arrange fish in shallow dish. In another bowl, combine oil, vinegar, salt, paprika, garlic and cayenne; pour over fish. Cover and refrigerate at least 2 hours, turning several times. Place steaks on lightly-oiled broiler pan, reserving marinade for basting. In a small saucepan, heat marinade to boiling; remove from heat. Broil steaks approximately 3 inches from broiler unit for 6-8 minutes, basting with marinade. Turn steaks, basting several times. Broil and additional 6-8 minutes or until fish flakes easily with a fork. Discard marinade. Sprinkle with paprika and chopped parsley. Serves 6.

Viva l' Tilapia

1/4 cup chopped **Celery**
1/4 cup chopped **Onions**
1/3 cup chopped **Red Bell Pepper**
3 tbsp. **Butter**
3 tbsp. **All-Purpose Flour**
1/2 tsp. **Salt**
1/4 tsp. **Pepper**

1/2 tsp **Tarragon**
1/2 tsp. **Basil**
1 1/4 cups **Milk**
1 cup shredded **Mozzarella Cheese**
1 1/2 lbs. **Tilapia Fillets**

Preheat oven to 450 degrees. In a medium skillet, sauté celery, onions and bell pepper in butter until tender. Add flour, salt, pepper, tarragon, basil and milk; mix well. Cook for 1 minute, stirring constantly until thickened. Add cheese and stir until melted. Do not boil. Place fillets in a 12 x 8 baking dish and spoon sauce over top. Bake for 8-10 minutes or until fish flakes easily with a fork. Serves 4.

Herb-Seasoned Shark Steaks

2 lbs. **Shark Steaks**
1 tsp. **Salt**
1/4 tsp. **White Pepper**
Juice of 1 **Lime**

1/2 tsp. **Thyme Leaves**
1 tsp. minced **Garlic**
1/2 cup chopped **Green Onions**
2 **Tomatoes**, sliced

Preheat oven to 375 degrees. Sprinkle salt and pepper on both sides of shark steaks and arrange in a shallow baking dish. Pour lime juice over fish and sprinkle with thyme, garlic and onions. Top fish with sliced tomatoes. Bake for 20-25 minutes or until fish flakes easily with a fork. Serves 6.

Side Dishes

Mushroom Casserole

"This casserole dish is one that my family always requests for our holiday dinners and family gatherings. It is easy to make and there are never any leftovers!"

Eleanor Harness—Sebring

25 **Soda Crackers**, crumbled
1/2 stick **Margarine**, melted
4 cans (4.5 oz. ea.) **Mushrooms**,
    two cans drained

1 medium **Onion**, diced
2 **Eggs**, beaten
4 oz. **Velveeta**®, cubed
1/2 cup **Milk**

Pre-heat oven to 350 degrees. In a medium mixing bowl, combine all ingredients and mix well. Pour into a greased 1 1/2-quart casserole dish. Bake, covered, for 25 minutes, then remove cover and continue to bake for 20 minutes.

Caribbean Corn & Vegetable Bake

Florida Supersweet Corn Council, Tallahassee

2 tbsp. **Oil**
   Corn,
2 1/2 tsp. ground **Cumin**
1 tsp. **Salt**
3/4 tsp. **Sugar**
3/4 tsp. crumbled dried **Thyme**
1/2 tsp. ground **Black Pepper**
1/8 tsp. ground **Red Pepper**

4 ears fresh **Supersweet**
   shucked and halved
1 lb. **Plum Tomatoes**,
   halved
2 1/2 cups quartered small
   Potatoes
2 medium **Onions**, cut
   into thin wedges

Preheat oven to 450 degrees. In a small bowl, mix together oil, cumin, salt, sugar, thyme, black pepper and red pepper until blended. Place corn, tomatoes, potatoes and onions in a 15 X10 roasting pan. Pour the oil mixture over the vegetables; toss gently to coat. Cover pan with foil. Bake, stirring once or twice, until vegetables are tender, about 30 minutes. Serves 4-6.

John Ringling selected this city for his Ringling Brothers and Barnum & Bailey Circus and made it his home in the late 1920s. The Ringling residence, Ca' d'Zan, is a 30-room mansion that resembles a Venetian palace. This beach resort and art community includes the offshore islands of Siesta Key, St. Armand Key, Longboat Key and Lido Key.

Zucchini Supreme

"My sister developed this wonderful recipe."

Sylvia D. Owens — Williston

1 tbsp. **Soy Sauce**
6 **Egg Whites**
3 cups shredded unpeeled **Zucchini**
3/4 cup **Whole-Wheat Flour**
1/4 cup toasted **Wheat Germ**
1/2 cup shredded **Parmesan Cheese**
1/2 cup finely chopped **Onion**

2 tbsp. chopped fresh **Parsley**
1/2 tsp. **Italian Seasoning**
2 cloves **Garlic,** minced
1 tsp. **Butter Flavored Salt**
1/2 tsp. **Pepper**
1 tsp. **Baking Soda**

Preheat oven to 350 degrees. Prepare a 13 X9 casserole dish with cooking spray. In a bowl, beat soy sauce and egg whites until peaks form. In a separate bowl, combine remaining ingredients, blend well and fold into egg white mixture. Gently pour into casserole dish. Bake for 25-30 minutes or until slightly brown on top. Cut into squares and serve warm. Serves 8.

Stuffed Bananas

This recipe is from the Historic Spanish Point: Cooking Then and Now cookbook.

Gulf Coast Heritage Association, Inc.0—Osprey.

6 large **Bananas**
2 1/2 cups mashed **Yams**
1 tbsp. **Brown Sugar**

1 tsp. **Salt**
3 strips of **Bacon**, cooked
    crisp and crumbled

Pre-heat oven to 350 degrees. Split unpeeled bananas lengthwise without cutting all the way through. Remove as much banana pulp as possible, combine pulp with the yams and mix well. Stir in brown sugar, salt and bacon, then stuff mixture into the banana skins. Bake for 20 minutes.

Zucchini Puff

"I am 75-years-old and I can still remember my grandmother, a western settler, serving this dish. It is easy to prepare and contains ordinary ingredients that a farmer then would have had as easily available to him as we do today."

Helen L. Johnson—Sanibel

2 1/2 tbsp. **Butter**
1 medium **Onion**, sliced in thin rings
2 medium **Zucchini,** cut in 1/2-inch slices
4 large **Eggs**
2 tbsp. **Water**
Salt and **Pepper** to taste
1/2 cup shredded **Cheddar** or **Swiss Cheese**

Preheat broiler to 400 degrees. In a large heavy skillet, melt 2 tablespoons butter. Add onion and sauté until just translucent. Add zucchini and continue to cook, stirring occasionally, until onions and zucchini are slightly browned. In a small mixing bowl, beat eggs with water, add salt and pepper and stir into zucchini mixture. Cook on medium heat until the eggs are half-cooked and the bottom of the eggs are barely done. Run extra butter around the rim of the skillet, sprinkle the cheddar cheese on top of the eggs and place the skillet under the broiler. Watch carefully—the soufflé will puff up, the cheese will melt and the top will turn golden. Serve immediately. Serves 4.

Sanibel Island

It is said that the pirate, Jose Gaspar, was named Sanibel after the beautiful queen of Spain, Santa Isabella. He is also supposed to have kept his favorite captive women on Captiva, a small island just north of Sanibel. Sanibel's beaches are well-known to be among the best in the world for shell collecting. Visit the Bailey-Mathews Shell Museum or take a wildlife drive through the 6,000 acre J.N. "Ding" Darling National Wildlife refuge.

Carrot Souffle

"This recipe was given to me by my mother and is a traditional holiday dish in our family. Carrots grow well in North Central Florida gardens and free-range chicken eggs are plentiful, too."

Drollene P. Brown—A+ Writing, Morriston

4 **Eggs**
2 cups cooked **Carrots**
1/2 stick **Butter**
1 cup **Milk**

1/4 cup **Sugar**
2 tbsp. **Flour**
1 tsp. **Baking Powder**
1 tsp. **Cinnamon**

Topping

1 cup packed **Brown Sugar**
1/2 stick + 1 tbsp. **Butter**

1/3 cup **Flour**
1 cup chopped **Pecans**

Preheat oven to 450 degrees. Prepare a deep casserole or soufflé dish with cooking spray. In a bowl, beat eggs until fluffy and set aside. In another bowl, mash carrots and butter together, mix in beaten eggs, milk, sugar, flour, baking powder and cinnamon and pour into casserole dish. Bake for 10 minutes, reduce oven temperature to 350 degrees and bake for 35 minutes. In a small mixing bowl, combine ingredients for topping and mix well, Remove soufflé from oven and sprinkle with topping. Return to oven for an additional 15-30 minutes.

Mom's Cornbread Casserole

"This is a family recipe from my mother-in-law. We serve it often for company and holidays meals."

Sylvia D. Owens—Williston

1 cup **Cornmeal**
3 tsp. **Baking Powder**
1/2 tsp. **Salt**
3 large **Eggs**

1 can (15oz.) **Cream-Style Corn**
1 cup **Sour Cream**
1/4 cup **Vegetable Oil**

Preheat oven to 450 degrees. Grease a 13 X 9 casserole dish and set aside. In a bowl, sift cornmeal, baking powder and salt together. Stir in eggs, corn, sour cream and oil and pour batter into the prepared casserole dish. Bake for 25 minutes. Serves 8-10.

Superb Spinach

"My sister gave me this recipe. It is good for anyone, especially those who think they don't like spinach (like my husband!)"

Margaret Friedling—St. Petersburg

1/2 cup **Butter**, melted
2 packages (10 oz. ea.) frozen, chopped **Spinach**
2 lbs. small curd **Cottage Cheese**
12 slices **Old English®️ Cheese**, cut into pieces
3 tbsp. **All-Purpose Flour**

6 **Eggs**
3 tbsp. **Lemon Juice**
2 tsp. **Salt**
1/2 tsp. **Pepper**
1/4 tsp. **Nutmeg**
6 slices **Bacon**, cooked and crumbled

Pre-heat oven to 325 degrees. In a skillet, heat 4 tablespoonfuls of the butter, add spinach and cook just until thawed. Place spinach, cottage cheese and Old English cheese in a blender. Turn blender on and off several times until mixture is just blended. In a medium mixing bowl, combine remaining butter, flour, eggs, lemon juice and spices and mix well. Stir in spinach and cheese mixture and pour into an 11 X 9 casserole dish. Bake for 30 minutes, sprinkle top with crumbled bacon and bake for 15 minutes more.

Mary Grey's Mango Chutney

"This recipe has been in our family for 60 years. It takes half a day to make but it's worth it!"

Lindsay Richards—Mount Dora Historic Inn, Mount Dora

8 cups peeled diced **Mango**
16 oz. **Grapefruit Juice**
16 oz. **Vinegar**
1 1/2 cups chopped **Onion**
1 cup chopped **Apple**
1 1/2 pounds **Brown Sugar**
1 large **Green Bell Pepper**, chopped
6 small **Jalapeno Peppers**, chopped
1 lb. **Currants**

1/4 cup chopped fresh **Ginger**
1/2 tsp. grated fresh **Lime Rind**
2 tbsp. fresh **Lime Juice**
3/4 tsp. **Salt**
1 tsp. ground **Cinnamon**
3/4 tsp. ground **Cloves**
1 tbsp. **Mustard Seed**
1 1/2 tsp. **Celery Seed**

In a large saucepan or Dutch oven, combine all ingredients and bring to a boil over medium heat. Reduce heat to simmer and cook for 1 1/2 hours, stirring occasionally. Carefully pour hot mixture into sterilized jars and seal.

Potato-Cheese Casserole

"A friend gave me this recipe many years ago. It is a great favorite of family and friends at gatherings and holiday meals. It goes well with any kind of meat and is easily doubled."

Eleanor Harness—Sebring

6 large **Potatoes**, unpeeled
4-5 **Green Onions**, chopped
Salt and **Pepper** to taste
1 stick **Margarine**

8 oz. **Cheddar Cheese**, grated
2 cups **Sour Cream**

Pre-heat oven to 350 degrees. In a large pot, boil potatoes until tender. Allow to cool, then grate unpeeled potatoes into a large mixing bowl. Add onion, salt and pepper and mix well. In a small saucepan, melt margarine, and pour over the potatoes. Mix cheddar cheese and sour cream together and stir into the potatoes. Spoon mixture into a shallow casserole dish. Bake for 45-50 minutes.

Rustic Tomato Tart in Basil Crust

*"You'll love the herb-flecked dough of this tart.
Serve with a colorful salad for a great meal."*

Alice Morton—Florida Tomato Committee, Orlando

Pastry:

1 1/4 cups **All-Purpose Flour**
2 tsp. dried **Basil**
1/4 tsp. **Salt**

1 stick **Butter,** cut into
   small pieces
1/4 cup **Cold Water** (4 tbsp.)

Filling:

3 tbsp. **Olive Oil**
3 cups thinly sliced **Onion**
1 clove **Garlic,** minced
1 tbsp. **Semolina Flour** or fine **Cornmeal**
2 large **Tomatoes,** cored and cut into 1/4-inch slices
Salt and freshly ground **Pepper** to taste
1 cup grated **Provolone** or **Mozzarella Cheese**

Combine flour, basil, salt and butter in a food processor or blender and blend for 10 seconds. Add 2 tablespoonfuls of the water and blend for 5 seconds. Add the remaining water and blend for 7 seconds or until the mixture forms damp crumbs. Place crumbs in a bowl and knead into a dough, adding drops of cold water as needed. Knead the dough for 1 minute. Flatten into a circle on a sheet of plastic wrap, then wrap and refrigerate for 30 minutes. In a large heavy skillet, heat olive oil, add the onion and sauté over low heat for 10-12 minutes, stirring occasionally, until golden brown. Add garlic and salt and sauté for 1 minute. Preheat oven to 400 degrees. Set onions aside to cool. Remove dough from refrigerator and roll into a 13-inch circle on a sheet of lightly-floured waxed paper, invert pastry onto a baking sheet and peel off the paper. Sprinkle the semolina flour onto the pastry in a 9-inch circle in the center. Spread onions over semolina flour and sprinkle 1/2 of the cheese on top. Arrange tomatoes in an overlapping circle over the onions, place slices in the center and sprinkle with salt and pepper. Fold the edges of the dough up over the filling, pleating it as you go. Bake on the center rack of the oven for 45 minutes. Slide the sheet out, cover tomatoes with the remaining provolone or mozzarella cheese and bake for 10 more minutes. Let cool on a wire rack for 10-15 minutes, then cut into wedges and serve. Serves 6-8.

Kumquat Chutney

This recipe is from the Historic Spanish Point: Cooking Then and Now cookbook

Gulf Coast Heritage Association, Inc.—Osprey

1 cup **Vinegar**
1 cup packed **Brown Sugar**
6 cups **Kumquats**, seeds removed
    sliced with juice
1 tbsp. **Lemon Juice**
2 cloves **Garlic**, minced
1/4 cup chopped **Ginger Root**
1 tsp. **Allspice**

1 tbsp. **Mustard Seed**
2 small **Apples**, peeled and
    chopped
1 tsp. **Salt**
1/2 tsp. **Red Pepper Flakes**
1 cup chopped **Onions**
1 tsp. ground **Cloves**
1 tsp. **Cinnamon**

In a large saucepan, combine vinegar and brown sugar and bring to a boil. Stir kumquats into mixture and reduce to a simmer. Add remaining ingredients, turn off heat and allow to cool. Bring to a simmer again and cook until desired thickness. Carefully pour mixture into hot sterilized jars and seal.

Earthquakes in Florida?

Experience an 8.3 earthquake that hurls fire and flood at Universal Studios Florida, just east of Orlando.

Passionate Plantains

Florida Tropical Fruit Growers of South Florida—Homestead

3-4 **Plantains**, peeled and sliced
Juice of 3 **Passion Fruit**
   (or 1/3 cup **Orange Juice**)
1 tbsp. **Butter**, melted

1/4 cup **Honey**
Juice and **Zest** of 1 **Lime**
1/2 tsp. **Nutmeg**

Pre-heat oven to 350 degrees, Arrange plantains in a glass baking dish. In a small mixing bowl, combine remaining ingredients and mix well. Sprinkle juice mixture over the top of the plantains. Bake for 30 minutes. Serve with chicken, port or brunch dishes. Serves 6-8.

Watermelon Pickles

*"I have tasted a few other watermelon pickles in my lifetime,
but none can compare to these!"*

Evelyn Evenson Pinther—Lake Wales

Watermelon Rind, from
   1 small watermelon
Non-Iodized Salt (very important)
7 1/2 cups **Sugar**

1 pint **White Vinegar**
1/2 tsp. **Oil of Cinnamon**
1/2 tsp **Oil of Cloves**
Maraschino Cherries, drained

Peel the watermelon rinds, slice to desired lengths and drain. In a large pot, cover rinds with water, add salt and boil until rinds are tender-crisp and almost translucent. Drain rinds, place in a large mixing bowl and set aside. In a saucepan, combine sugar and vinegar, bring to a boil and cook until sugar dissolves; add spice oils* and stir. Pour sugar mixture over the rinds, cover and allow to set. Each day, for three days, drain the syrup from the rinds, reheat syrup to boiling and pour back over the rinds. On the third day, place rinds and syrup in hot, sterilized jars and seal. For a dash of color, add a few maraschino cherries to each jar.

*Clove & cinnamon oils can be purchased from pharmacies.

Breads

Piña Colada Muffins

"This is one of our specialty recipes and a favorite of our guests."

Cindy Montalto—Magnolia Plantation Bed & Breakfast Inn, Gainesville

1 box (18.25 oz.) **Yellow** or **Butter Cake Mix**
1 tsp. **Coconut Extract**
1 tsp. **Rum Extract**
1 cup **Coconut Flakes**
1/2 -1 cup chopped **Nuts**
1 can (8oz.) crushed **Pineapple,** with juice

Pre-heat oven to 350 degrees. In a large mixing bowl, prepare cake mix following the instructions on the package. Add the remaining ingredients and stir for 1 minute. Pour batter into greased cups of 2 muffin tins to 3/4 full. Bake for 15-20 minutes or until golden brown. Makes 12 muffins.

Sabal Palm House Pumpkin Bread

"This is a favorite bread we serve to our guests."

Mike Breece—Sabla Palm House bred & Breakfast Inn, Lake Worth

3 1/3 cups **Flour**
3 cups **Sugar**
2 tsp. **Baking Soda**
1 1/2 tsp. **Salt**
3 tsp. **Cinnamon**
3 tsp. **Nutmeg**

1/2 tsp. ground **Cloves**
1 cup **Oil**
2/3 cup **Water**
4 **Eggs,** beaten
2 cups cooked or canned **Pumpkin**

Pre-heat oven to 350 degrees. In a large mixing bowl, combine all dry ingredients, mix well and form a "well" in the center. Add oil, water, eggs and pumpkin to the "well", then mix all ingredients thoroughly. Pour batter into 3 greased and floured loaf pans. Bake for 50-60 minutes.

Sweet Banana Bread

"I always loved my mother's recipe and have adapted it to serve my Tea Room guests. One of my guests won 1st prize at the Florida State Fair with it!"

Cavelle Pawlack—Meadow Marsh Bed & Breakfast, Orlando

2 cups **Flour**
1 tsp. **Baking Powder**
1 tsp. **Baking Soda**
3/4 tsp. **Salt**
1 1/3 cups **Sugar**
1/2 cup **Shortening**

1/2 cup **Sour Milk**
1 cup mashed **Bananas**
2 **Eggs**
1 tsp. **Vanilla**
1/2 cup chopped **Nuts**
1/2 cup **Raisins**

Pre-heat oven to 350 degrees. Combine all the ingredients in a large mixing bowl and mix well. Pour batter into a greased 9 x 5 loaf pan until 3/4 full. Pour any leftover into greased muffin cups. Bake for 45-55 minutes. If making muffins too, remove muffins after 18-20 minutes. Makes 1 loaf.

Avocado-Pecan Bread

This recipe is from the Historic Spanish Point: Cooking Then and Now cookbook.

Gulf Coast Heritage Association, Inc.—Osprey

1 cup **Sugar**	1 cup mashed, ripe **Avocado**
2 cups **All-Purpose Flour**	1 tbsp. **Vegetable Oil**
1/4 tsp **Salt**	1 tsp. grated **Lemon Rind**
1 tsp. **Baking Soda**	1 tsp. **Lemon Juice**
1/2 tsp. **Baking Powder**	1/2 tsp **Lemon Extract**
1 **Egg**, lightly beaten	3/4 cup chopped **Pecan**
1/2 cup **Buttermilk**	1/2 cup **Golden Raisins**

Pre-heat oven to 350 degrees. Sift sugar, flour, salt, baking soda and baking powder into a large mixing bowl. Add egg, buttermilk, avocado, oil, lemon rind, juice and extract, then beat well with mixer at medium speed. Fold in pecans and raisins. Spoon batter into a well- greased 9 x 5 loaf pan. Bake for 1 hour or until toothpick inserted in the center comes out clean. Cool in loaf pan for 10 minutes, remove and place on wire rack to cool completely. To prevent browning too quickly, place a pan of hot water on the top rack of the oven. Remove water 20 minutes before end of baking time. Makes 1 loaf.

Historic Spanish Point

This fascinating 30-acre site overlooking beautiful Little Sarasota Bay in Osprey preserves and interprets 5,000 years of history. Enter a prehistoric shell mound to experience an archaeology exhibition about this region's earliest inhabitants. Florida's pioneer life is shared through a homestead house, citrus packing house, chapel and pioneer cemetery. Also featured are formal gardens and lawns and nature trails that allow visitors to explore Florida's native plant communities.

Seminole Pumpkin Fry Bread

This recipe is from the Historic Spanish Point: Cooking Then and Now cookbook.

Gulf Coast Heritage Association, Inc.—Osprey

1 cup **Pumpkin Purée**   Dash of **Salt**
1 cup **Self-Rising Flour**   **Vegetable Oil**

Pour pumpkin purée into a large mixing bowl, then add flour and salt. More flour will be needed if purée is moist. When mixture holds together, place on a floured board and knead for several minutes. Divide dough into 2 or 3 parts; knead for several minutes. Divide dough into 2 or 3 parts; knead each into a roll, then cut into 1/4-inch slices. In a large iron skillet, heat oil and carefully add dough slices. Fry until brown on one side, then turn and brown the other side; slices will puff up and get crisp. Serve while hot. A small amount of brown sugar may be added if desired. Makes 18 small breads.

Gramma's Cracklin' Hoecake

"A truly Southern delite!"

Lucretia M. Morgan—Jacksonville

1/2 cup **Cracklins,**   3 heaping tbsp. **Cornmeal**
   broken into small pieces   1/2 tsp. **Salt**
1/2 cup **Hot Water**   **Water**, as needed

Preheat oven to 450 degrees. Soak cracklin's in hot water for 10 minutes. Add cornmeal, salt and enough water to make a very thin batter, similar to pancake batter. Pour batter into a greased 9-inch cake pan and bake for 5 minutes. Turn oven temperature down to 400 degrees and bake for another 15-20 minutes or until light brown.

Note: Cracklins are rendered pork or poultry fat, or the crisp, brown skin of fried or roasted pork. They can be found packaged in supermarkets and specialty markets.

Glazed Mango-Pecan Muffins

"The Cypress Inn is located along the bay front in Sarasota and was built in 1940 on historic property that was once a large mango grove. We have 12 mango trees that we harvest for use in our special culinary delights. During the mango season, we gather as many as 100 mangoes per day!"

Vicki Hadley, Robert and Nina Belott—The Cypress—
A Bed & Breakfast Inn, Sarasota

1/2 cup **Unsalted Butter**, softened	1 1/2 cups skinned and
3/4 cup **Sugar**	diced **Mango**
2 large **Eggs**	2 cups **Unbleached Flour**
1/2 cup **Sour Cream**	3/4 tsp. **Baking Powder**
1/2 cup **Milk**	1/2 tsp. **Baking Soda**
1 tsp. **Vanilla**	1/2 tsp. **Salt**
2 tbsp. **Lemon Zest**	1/2 cup chopped **Pecans**

Preheat oven to 375 degrees. In a large bowl, cream butter and sugar together. Beat in eggs, one at a time, then add sour cream, milk and vanilla and mix well. Stir in lemon zest and mango. In a medium bowl, mix flour, baking powder, baking soda and salt. Add flour mixture to creamed ingredients and stir until just moistened. Spoon batter into greased muffin cups and sprinkle tops with the pecans. Bake for 16-20 minutes, then allow to cook for 5 minutes. Drizzle muffins with **Rum Glaze Topping**. Serve warm. Makes 6 large or 12 regular muffins.

Rum Glaze Topping

1/2 cup **Powdered Sugar**	1 tbsp. **Dark Rum**
2 tbsp. fresh **Lemon Juice**	

Combine all ingredients in a small bowl.

Key Lime Bread

"The key lime tree is abundant in South Florida and we use its fruit in many ways. This bread is always a hit."

Sylvia D. Owens—Williston

2/3 cups **Butter** or **Margarine**, melted
1 3/4 cups **Sugar**
4 **Eggs**
1/2 tsp. **Vanilla**
2 medium **Key Limes**, rinds grated and juice reserved

3 cups **Flour**
3/4 tsp. **Salt**
2 1/2 tsp. **Baking Powder**
1 cup **Milk**
1 cup finely chopped **Pecans**

Preheat oven to 350 degrees. In a large mixing bowl, cream butter and sugar together, add in eggs, then vanilla and Key lime rind and stir until blended. In another bowl, combine flour, salt and baking powder and mix well. Add dry ingredients to creamed mixture alternately with milk. Fold in pecans. Pour batter into 2 greased loaf pans. Bake for 50-60 minutes. A few minutes before removing the loaves from the oven, prepare **Key Lime Glaze**. Allow loaves to cool for 1 minute. Spoon glaze over hot loaves while still in the pans, then allow to cool for 10 minutes. Remove loaves from pans and cool thoroughly. Wrap in parchment paper and store in a cool area for at least 24 hours before slicing.

Key Lime Glaze

Juice of 2 medium **Key Limes**   1/2 cup **Powdered Sugar**

Combine ingredients together in a bowl.

Did You Know?

The Sponge Fleet is blessed every year at Tarpon Springs with a colorful religious ceremony held at the Greek Orthodox Church of St. Nicholas. The sponge beds at Tarpon Springs were discovered in 1905.

Sunny Morning Bread

1 1/2 cups **Corn Flakes**
2 cups **Flour**
3 teaspoons **Baking Powder**
1/2 teaspoon **Salt**
1/2 cup softened **Butter**
1/2 cup **Sugar**
2 **Eggs**
1 tablespoon grated **Orange Rind**
1 cup **Orange Juice**
1/2 cup seedless **Raisins**
1/2 cup finely chopped **Nuts**

Measure corn flakes and crush to fill 3/4 cup. Set aside. Sift together flour, baking powder and salt. Set aside. Cream butter and sugar in mixing bowl until light and fluffy. Add eggs and orange rind and beat well. Stir in orange juice, mixing until well blended. Add flour mixture, stirring only until combined.

Stir in corn flakes, nuts and raisins. Spread in well-greased 9×5×3 pan. Bake in 350 degree oven about one hour. Cool in pan 10 minutes before removing. Set bread on wire rack to cool completely before slicing.

(To double the recipe, increase ingredients proportionately and bake in greased and floured 10-inch tube pan. Bake in 350 degree oven about 1 1/2 hours.)

Desserts

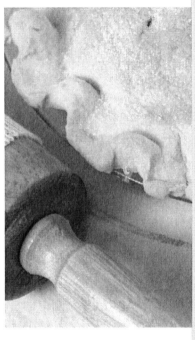

Aunt Sally's Key Lime Pie

*"This recipe was created by a lady known as Aunt Sally
who cooked for the Curry family in 1894."*

Edith Amsterdam—Curry Mansion Inn, Key West

4 **Eggs**, separated
1/2 cup **Key Lime Juice**
1 can (14 oz.) **Sweetened
Condensed Milk**

1 (8-inch) **Graham Cracker
Pie Crust**
1/4 tsp. **Cream of Tarter**
1/3 cup **Sugar**

Pre-heat oven to 350 degrees. In a medium mixing bowl, beat egg yolks until light and thick. Blend in lime juice and milk, stirring until mixture thickens. Pour mixture into the pie shell. In a medium mixing bowl, beat egg whites with cream of tarter until stiff, gradually beat in sugar and continue beating until glossy peaks form. Spread egg whites over the surface of the pie to the edge of the crust. Bake for 20 minutes or until golden brown. Chill before serving.

DePalma's Devilish Delights

(AKA: Jalapeño Brownies with Chocolate Crème Frosting)

"This is my mother's brownie recipe, I added the peppers and renamed it. 10 jalapeños may seem scary, but that's what I use. Of course, the 'hotness' may vary from pepper to pepper."

M. E. De Palma—National Hot Pepper Assoc., Ft. Lauderdale

10 **Jalapeño Peppers**
1 cup **Semi-Sweet**
   Chocolate Chips
1/4 lb. **Butter**
4 **Eggs**

1/3 tsp. **Salt**
2 cups **Sugar**
1 tsp. **Vanilla**
1 1/4 cups **Flour**
1 cup **Nuts**

Pre-heat oven to 350 degrees. Clean, devein and finely chop jalapeños. In a double boiler, melt chocolate chips and butter. In a bowl, beat eggs until foamy; add salt and sugar and beat until well-blended. Stir in vanilla and chocolate mixture. Add flour and stir until lightly blended. Fold in jalapeños and nuts. Butter bottom and sides of a 13 x 9 pan and add brownie mixture. Bake for 25 to 30 minutes. When cool, frost with **Chocolate Crème Frosting**.

Chocolate Crème Frosting

8 oz. **Cream Cheese**
1/4 lb. **Butter**
1 tsp. **Vanilla**

4 tbsp. **Cream**
3 tbsp. **Cocoa**
3 cups **Powdered Sugar**

In a bowl, blend cream cheese and butter with a mixer. Add vanilla and cream and combine. Add cocoa and powdered sugar and blend well.

St. Petersburg

Located on the Tampa Bay coast, this well-known tourist destination is famous world wide. Miles of sandy beaches ensure a great outdoor experience. Downtown, The Pier is a west coast landmark, and a visit to the Salvador Dali Museum provides a memorable experience.

Floridian Citrus Cup

"This is a Florida treat for a hot, humid day."

Fran Bennett—Sebring

2 large **Oranges**, cut in half
2 **Egg Whites**
2 tbsp. **Sugar**

1 tsp. **Vanilla**
4 tsp. **Red Wine**

Scoop pulp out of each of the orange halves, divide into bite-size chunks and set aside. Cut a tiny slice off the bottom of each "cup" to stabilize. In a large bowl, combine egg whites, sugar and vanilla and whisk until peaks form. Place a teaspoonful of red wine in each of the cups; add a few chunks of orange to each and spoon egg white mixture over top. Place orange halves in a shallow baking pan and broil for 1 minute; serve warm.

The Sunshine Skyway Bridge

This 4.1 mile concrete bridge coasts through the clouds at 190 feet above Tampa Bay, connecting St. Petersburg to the mainland and Highway 75 south to Sarasota.

Strawberry Compote

"Nearby Plant City is called the 'Strawberry Capital of the World.'
Thanks to our wonderful weather, we have fresh strawberries several months of the year. This recipe is pretty delicious and nutritious. I have made it for almost 50 years!"

Evelyn Evensen Pinther—Lake Wales

2 boxes (10 oz. ea.) frozen sliced **Strawberries**
2 large cans (20 oz.) **Pineapple Chunks**, drained
2 cans (11 oz. ea.) **Mandarin Oranges**, drained
2 **Bananas**, sliced

In a medium mixing bowl, combine all the ingredients, except bananas, and mix gently. Cover and refrigerate until thoroughly chilled. Just before serving, add bananas and stir. Serves 10.

Bread Pudding with Caramel Sauce

"This is a delicious variation on traditional bread puddings."

Terry Jackson—St. Francis Inn, St. Augustine

1 loaf day-old **Bread, Rolls**
  or **Muffins**
1 1/2 cups **Milk**
1/2 cup **Sugar**
3 tsp. **Cinnamon**
2 tsp. **Vanilla**
1 tsp. **Almond Extract**

1 cup chopped **Pecans**
8 **Eggs**, beaten
2 cups diced **Apples**
1 **Banana**, diced
Brown Sugar
1/2 cup **Butter**

Cut bread into 2-inch pieces and place in a bowl, add milk and soak thoroughly. In another bowl, combine sugar, cinnamon, vanilla, almond extract, pecans, eggs, apples and banana and mix well. Spread 1/2 of the bread on the bottom of a 2-quart baking dish. Add a layer of half of the sugar mixture, sprinkle top with brown sugar and dot with 1/2 of the butter. Repeat layers. Bake for 1 to 1 1/2 hours. Serve with **Caramel Sauce** drizzled over top.

Caramel Sauce

1 box (16 oz.) **Light Brown Sugar**
1/2 cup **Water**
1 cup **Heavy Cream**

In a heavy saucepan, melt brown sugar in water and bring to a boil. Reduce heat, stir in heavy cream and simmer until thickened and glossy.

Jacksonville

Covering 840 square miles, this is the largest city in Florida and the second largest in the U.S. (Juneau, Alaska is first). Founded in 1822, the year after the U.S. took formal possession of Florida from Spain, this city was named after General Andrew Jackson who later became the 7th president of the U.S.

Orange Meringue Pie

"I made up this recipe by combining two other recipes and came up with this one which I really like."

1/4 cup **Cornstarch**
1 cup **Sugar.**
1 3/4 cup + 6 tbsp. fresh **Orange Juice**

3 **Eggs**, separated
1 tbsp. **Margarine** or **Butter**
1 tbsp. grated **Orange Rind**
1 (9-inch) baked **Pie Shell**

Preheat oven to 400 degrees. In a saucepan, combine cornstarch, 1 cup of sugar and 3/4 cup of the orange juice and mix well. In a bowl, beat egg yolks, add to the cornstarch mixture and then stir in the remaining orange juice. Bring mixture to a boil, reduce heat and simmer for 5 minutes, stirring constantly. Remove from heat, add margarine and orange rind and stir until margarine has melted and mixture is well-blended. Pour into the pie shell. In a bowl, beat egg whites with electric mixer at high speed until soft peaks form. Gradually add 6 tbsp. sugar and continue to beat at high speed until stiff glossy peaks form. Spread meringue over the filling, carefully sealing to edges. Bake for 8-10 minutes or until brown. Cool on a wire rack and refrigerate.

Bernice's Custard

"Just a good old-fashioned favorite."

Clare Heiser—Lantana

8 cups **Milk**
8 **Egg Yolks**
4 cups **Sugar**

Dash of **Salt**
1 tbsp. **Vanilla**

In a small saucepan, scald milk. In a bowl, beat egg yolks, add sugar and combine. Pour hot milk over the mixture, then pour into a double boiler and cook until the mixture thickens. Allow mixture to cool, then stir in salt and vanilla. Chill and serve.

Loquat Pie

"The loquat is also called a Japanese plum. They are the sweetest when golden ripe. Be very careful in measuring the spices as even a bit too much will make this taste like an apple pie!"

Alice Koster—Lake Placid

4 cups **Loquats**, peeled and seeded
2 (9-inch) unbaked **Pie Crusts**
2/3 cup **Sugar**
1 1/2 tbsp. quick-cooking
    Tapioca
1/2 tsp. grated **Lemon Rind**

1-2 tsp. **Lemon Juice**
1/4 tsp. **Nutmeg**
1/2 tsp. **Cinnamon**
1/8 tsp. **Salt**
Butter
Sugar

Pre-heat oven to 425 degrees. Layer 1/2 of the loquats in pie shell. Combine balance of ingredients and sprinkle 1/2 of the mixture over loquats. Repeat layers and then dot top with butter. Add top crust and sprinkle with sugar. Bake for 40-50 minutes or until fruit is tender. Let cool thoroughly before serving.

Southern Pecan Pie

"Pecan pie is one of my husband's favorites. After trying several recipes, I came up with this version and he loves it!"

Mary Lou Meek—Sebring

1 cup **Pecan Halves**
1 (9-inch) unbaked **Pie Shell**
3 **Eggs**
1 tbsp. **Butter** or **Margarine**,
    melted

1 cup **Light Corn Syrup**
1/2 tsp. **Vanilla**
1 cup **Sugar**
1 tbsp. **Flour**

Pre-heat oven to 350 degrees. Place pecans in the bottom of pie shell. In a medium mixing bowl, beat eggs, add butter, corn syrup and vanilla and stir until well-blended. Gradually add sugar and flour to egg mixture and mix well. Pour mixture over the pecans and let stand until pecans rise to the top. Bake for 45 minutes.

Grandmother's Tea Cakes

"This is the recipe for my grandmother Clifford's tea cakes. They were served with afternoon tea when I was a little girl (more than 80 years ago!) I use the same recipe now to make cookies."

Betty Canaday—Melrose

1 cup **Butter**, softened	3 1/2 cups **Flour**
2 cups packed **Brown Sugar**	1 tsp. **Baking Soda**
2 **Eggs**, beaten	1/2 tsp. **Salt**

Pre-heat oven to 325 degrees. In a large mixing bowl, cream butter and brown sugar together, add eggs and blend. Sift flour, baking soda and salt three times, then add to creamed mixture and mix well. Pat dough out on waxed paper to about 1/2-inch thickness and use a cookie cutter to cut out shapes. Place cookies on a lightly-greased baking sheet. Bake for 8 minutes or until edges begin to brown; cookies will be flat and crispy. Allow to cool slightly before removing from sheet.

Lillian's Dump Cake

"I have made this cake for 25 years and have even won a church bake-off with it. It is easy and fun to make. I freeze the fruits and berries I grow, then use them in this cake."

Lillian Madden—Willsiton

1 stick **Margarine**	2 cups **Milk**
2 cups **Sugar**	1/4 cup **Oil**
2 cups **Self-Rising Flour**	2 cups frozen **Fruit,** any kind

Preheat oven to 450 degrees. Place cake pan in oven, add margarine and let it melt. In a large mixing bowl, combine sugar, flour, milk and oil and mix well. While pan is still in the oven, open the door and "dump" the sugar mixture into the pan on top of the margarine. Do not mix. Dump: frozen fruit on top of the batter, then close oven door. Bake for 35-45 minutes. The cake will have a caramel crust with partially cooked fruit and the bottom will be like a custard. Serve with ice cream or whipped cream while hot.

Tangy Truffles

"If you are a 'chocolate' and a 'chile-head' you'll love these melt-in-your-mouth chocolate truffles. They have a pleasant zing, which you will notice shortly after your first taste. Best of all, this recipe is easy to prepare!"

Herald & Renat Zoschke—Suncoast Peppers, Inc. St. Petersburg

6 oz. **Semi-Sweet Chocolate Bars** or **Chips**, high quality
1/3 cup **Whipping Cream**
1/2 tsp. natural **Vanilla Extract**
4 tsp. **Florida Heat® Hot Sauce**

If using chocolate bars, break into small pieces. Place chocolate in the top half of a double broiler. Add water to the bottom half and heat to just below boiling; turn off heat. In a small saucepan, heat cream to a quick boil and stir in the vanilla and hot sauce; let cool for 5 minutes. When chocolate has completely melted, whisk until smooth. Add the cream mixture to the chocolate and mix for 2 minutes or until well-blended. Pour the mixture into confectioner's cups or a buttered 8 x 8 baking pan and refrigerate for 2 hours. If chilled in a pan, cut cold truffle into small pieces. Refrigerate truffles in an airtight container for 1 week or freeze for up to 2 months.

Lime & Lychee Ice

Florida Tropical Fruit Growers of South Florida—Homestead

1 lb. fresh **Lychees,** peeled and seeded
Juice of 1 **Lime**
3/4 cup **Powdered Sugar,** sifted
Fresh **Mango, Papaya** or other **Tropical Fruit,** sliced for garnish

In a blender, combine lychee flesh, lime juice and powdered sugar and process until smooth. Pour into a suitable freezer container and freeze mixture until slushy, then beat well. Repeat this process twice, then freeze for several hours until solid. Serve in small scoops with slices of fresh mango, papaya or other tropical fruit. Serves 4.

Chalet Suzanne's Orange Aspic Pound Cake

"Since the 1950's, Chelte Sauzanne has produced a line of gourmet soups and sauces. This recipe is one of he most requested."

Vita Hinshaw—Chalet Suzanne Restaurant & Inn, Lake Wales

4 **Eggs**
1 package (18.25 oz.) **Yellow Cake Mix**
1 cup **Chalet Suzanne® Orange Aspic**
1 package (3.75 oz.) **Vanilla Instant Pudding Mix**
2/3 cup **Water**
1/4 cup **Cooking Oil**

Preheat oven to 325 degrees. In a small bowl, lightly beat eggs. In a large bowl, combine remaining cake ingredients, add eggs and beat with electric mixer for 2 minutes at medium speed. Pour batter into a greased and floured 9-inch Bundt pan. Bake for 45 minutes or until toothpick inserted in center of cake comes out clean. Allow to cool for 10-15 minutes before removing from pan. Drizzle **Orange Aspic Glaze** over top and sides of cake.

Orange Aspic Glaze

1/2 cup **Chalet Suzanne® Orange Aspic**
1 tbsp. **Butter** or **Margarine**
2 cups **Powdered Sugar**

In a small saucepan, warm aspic over low heat until thinned. Add butter and heat until butter has melted. Blend in powdered sugar.

Tampa

In the 1880's, a mining and shipping boom began with the discovery of phosphates in this area. Tampa is now the 7th largest shipping port in the world. Area attractions include Busch Gardens Tampa Bay and the three-story glass-domed Florida Aquarium. The world's first scheduled airline service, St. Petersburg-Tampa Airboat Line, was established in 1914 by P. E. Fansler.

Thick & Rich Hot Fudge Sauce

"This is great on ice cream, biscuits, pound cakes and honey buns."

Shirley A. Tapley—Bonifay

4 squares (1 oz. ea.) **Semi-Sweet Chocolate**
2 tbsp. **Butter**
1 tsp. **Vanilla**
1 can (14 oz.) **Eagle Brand® Sweetened Condensed Milk**
Dash of **Salt**

In a small saucepan, melt chocolate and butter over low heat, then stir in vanilla, condensed milk and salt. Cook, stirring constantly, for 3-5 minutes until thick and smooth.

Sunshine Cake

"As my age increased and metabolism rate decreased, I had to find an alternative to rum cake. This is it!"

Carol Johnston—Greenwood

1 can (11oz.) **Mandarin Oranges**, with juice
1 package (18.25 oz.) **Yellow Cake Mix**
1/2 cup **Applesauce**
4 **Eggs**

Frosting:

1 can (20 oz.) crushed **Pineapple,** with juice
1 package (18 oz.) **Sugar-Free Instant Vanilla Pudding Mix**

Preheat oven to 350 degrees. Pour oranges from can into a bowl, sort through and remove sectional strands. Add cake mix, applesauce and eggs and beat until well-blended. Pour batter into a 13 x 9 cake pan that has been sprayed with cooking spray. Bake for 35 minutes or until toothpick inserted in center of cake comes out clean. Allow to cool completely. In a small bowl, combine pineapple, juice and pudding mix and stir well. Spread over top of cake. Store in refrigerator.

Kumquat Refrigerator Pie

Roxine Barthle—Katy's Country Corner, St. Joseph

1 carton (8 oz.) frozen **Whipped Topping**
1 can (14 oz.) **Sweetened Condensed Milk**
1/2 cup fresh **Lemon Juice**
2/3 cup puréed **Kumquats**
1 (9-inch) **Graham Cracker** or baked **Pie Crust**
Fresh **Kumquats** and **Mint Leaves**, for garnish

Combine and beat the whipped topping and condensed milk. Add lemon juice and beat until thickened. Add puréed kumquats and stir. Pour mixture into pie shell and chill in refrigerator. Garnish with fresh kumquats and mint leaves.

Puréed Kumquats

Wash fruit, cut in half and remove seeds. Place in a blender and purée until smooth. Purée can be frozen and stored for six months. Defrost and drain liquid before using.

Kumquat Oatmeal Cookies

"St. Joseph is called the Kumquat Capital of the world! In this area, more kumquats are grown than anywhere in the U.S.!"

Rosemary GudeKumquat Growers of Saint Joseph, Saint Joseph

2/3 cup **Margarine**
2/3 cups packed **Brown Sugar**
2 large **Eggs**
1 1/2 cups **Oatmeal**
2 cups **Flour**

1 tsp. **Baking Soda**
1 tsp. **Salt**
2/3 cup **Puréed Kumquats**
2/3 cup **White Chocolate Chips**

Pre-heat oven to 375 degrees. Beat margarine and sugar until fluffy. Add eggs and mix well. Add in the oatmeal, flour, baking soda and salt, mixing well. Add kumquats and chocolate chips. Drop by large teaspoonful onto un-greased cookie sheets. Bake for 10-15 minutes or until golden brown.

If you love cookbooks, then you'll love these too!

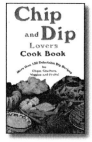

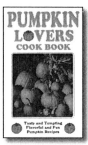

QTY	TITLE	PRICE	TOTAL
	Burrito Lovers' Cook Book	9.95	
	Chili Lovers' Cook Book	9.95	
	Chip & Dip Lovers' Cook Book	9.95	
	Citrus Lovers' Cook Book	9.95	
	Easy BBQ Recipes	9.95	
	Easy BBQ Sauces	9.95	
	Grand Canyon Cook Book	9.95	
	Low Fat Mexican Recipes	9.95	
	New Mexico Cook Book	9.95	
	Mexican Family Favorites Cook Book	9.95	
	Quick-n-Easy Mexican Recipes	9.95	
	Salsa Lovers' Cook Book	9.95	
	Sedona Cook Book	9.95	
	Tequila Cook Book	9.95	
	Texas Cook Book	9.95	
	Tortilla Lovers' Cook Book	9.95	
	Veggie Lovers' Cook Book	9.95	
	Western Breakfast	9.95	

US Shipping & Handling Add	1-3 Books: 5.00	
[for non-domestic ship rates, please call]	4-9 Books: 7.00	
	9+ Books: 7.00 + 0.25 per book	
	AZ residents add 8.3% sales tax	
	(US funds only) Total:	

Please make checks payable to:
Golden West Publishers
4113 N. Longview,
Phoenix, AZ 85014

☐ Check or money order enclosed
☐ MC ☐ VISA ☐ Discover ☐ American Express Verification Code:_____

Card Number:_____ Exp._____

Signature: _____

Name_____Phone: _____

Address _____

City_____State_____ZIP _____

Email _____

Prices are subject to change.

Visit our website or call us toll free for a free catalog of all our titles!